I0617948

The Necessity of All Things

In Order to Come Full Circle with Your Purpose You Must Understand Your Lifescript

Allenda Felice Henry

The Reading Glass
BOOKS

The Necessity of All Things
Copyright © 2023 by Allenda Felice Henry

All rights reserved. No part of this publication may be reproduced, distributed, or transmitted in any form or by any means, including photocopying, recording, or other electronic or mechanical methods, without the prior written permission of the publisher or author, except in the case of brief quotations embodied in critical reviews and certain other noncommercial uses permitted by copyright law.

ISBN:
(Paperback)   978-1959151524
(e-book)   978-1959151531

The views expressed in this book are solely those of the author and do not necessarily reflect the views of the publisher, and the publisher hereby disclaims any responsibility for them.

The Reading Glass Books
1-888-420-3050
www.readingglassbooks.com
production@readingglassbooks.com

Contents

At the request of the author no further editing was completed. The author is not seeking perfection with her first book, but rather transparency and authenticity of her spiritual journey. She insists on revealing her flaws and imperfections, as this was a part of awakening.

"Humility is the solid foundation of all virtues."
"We come nearest to the universe when we are great in humility."
"True humility is intelligent self-respect which keeps us from thinking too highly or too meanly of ourselves. It makes us modest by reminding us of how far we have come short of what we can be."

– Xavier University,

u

Foreword

I've known Allenda for about one year, we met at a Coffee House on the Windward side of Oahu. Upon our initial meeting I felt an immediate connection, I now know it was spiritual, I can't explain it but what I can say is that this woman has truly been a favorable blessing to me. Prior to our meeting we would run into each other everyday for coffee, she captured my attention because of her beauty and how well dressed she presented herself, I thought she was a physician or some type of an Executive because she was always put together so well and she smelled like a fragrance from one of those high end stores that you wanted to know where the scent was coming from because it grabbed your attention, the aroma of it was so inviting but you knew it cost too much to purchase for yourself so you just take in the scent and proceed to the person wearing this amazing fragrance and ask "excuse me but what are you wearing"? Allenda would speak to everyone who was in line and she always had a smile, I even witnessed her pay in advance for the next two or three people that would come in for coffee and she would never share that she was the one who paid, and this blew me away. I've heard of individuals who would pay it forward but never actually witnessed it and I was impressed.

For those of you that don't know her, she has this striking presence when you see her, she's a very attractive woman, beautifully dressed, and classy. She has a very humble and inviting aura and it will grab your attention especially her beautiful smile and lovely disposition. Whenever I would see her, she was always happy and it appeared genuine. I finally decided to approach her and asked "are you happy everyday"? Unaware that this question would begin the development of a friendship and my own spiritual journey that would transform me and my life. This chance meeting forge a friendship between us forever!

The conversation that took place between us was unforgettable and inspirational. As we began to speak she shared her story and it initiated an awaken that prompted a spark that reignited a dark part of my life that I thought I had forgotten about, something that was so deep within my subconscious, I assumed I had buried this ugliness a long time ago, which was my past. These types of emotions or connections didn't exist for me because of how my life had taken on so many different twists and turns that my existence no longer belonged to me. I had lost that woman long ago. The majority of my decisions were based on the needs of others and not my own I never truly thought about my purpose, I never gave it a second thought. I had placed the needs of my brothers and sisters before my own, because I believed I had no other choice. My parents were drug addicts and we never knew how or what a mom or dad were supposed to look like or be, we only knew what existed in our world. As I grew older our living situation increasingly got worse, there were days that we had no lights, water, or food and my parents were nowhere to be found, so I had to make a decision to do whatever necessary to ensure that my brothers and sisters were able to eat. The choices I made were based on survival. I'm not proud of my past but it was necessary in order for us to see another day. I had forgotten about this aspect of my life, I had buried these memories so deep that to think of my past only brought about bad memories of choices made out of desperation.

Nonetheless, she continued to share with me what brought her to Hawaii but what I believed to be so profound with our conversation was the story of her father's death and how his transition from this life brought about her transformation. Unbeknownst to me Allenda would prove to be more than a friend, she was the missing link that helped me to find and unlock my purpose. Upon meeting her I didn't realize that she worked in healthcare, and now I'm convinced that our meeting wasn't by chance, this would all prove that it's true what they say, there's no such thing as coincidences, or accidents, everything happens for a reason, the chances of two people intersecting paths was meant to be.

I shared with her that I never believed in these types of things, but I do now. I shared with her that I also worked in healthcare for many years, and I've witnessed so much disparity, death, drugs, alcohol and unthinkable addictions, the elderly who had been left alone by family to meet their fate unloved, the homeless, the young and their reckless behavior and those who had been abused by family, this was a world in which I came from and I craved to fit into this type of environment because I could relate to it and I would be capable of not displaying any emotional bonds with people. Unfortunately, overtime this can create a person to develop a hardened heart, thick skin and this came easy for me because of my past life. I've had people to say to me that this may be perceived as being cold or rude but what most don't realize or understand is that this was a world in which I lived for so long. I believed I chose healthcare because of the contrariety similarities that took place in my life, the tragedy and incongruity didn't bother me, but looking back on this now this wasn't a normal way to perceive life. I had developed an altered perception of reality, my skin had become more than just thick and it caused me to become desensitized from being human at times.

Whenever I saw Allenda I would watch her and how she interacted with people, and this amazed me. I wanted that same kind of connection with people. When she speaks to you, you are automatically drawn into the beauty of her smile, her laughter is infectious and it draws you in wanting more. She has a way of making you feel really good about whatever it is that you are going through, she gives off good energy and when I asked her how could she be so happy everyday she smiled and took the time to explain to me that there is no other way. She shared the steps she took towards achieving her happiness and because of this she is able to stand so strong in her faith and confident in her truth.

You see today's people don't bother to take time to listen to your struggles or hard times, everyone has an agenda, out to get or absorbed what ever they can in order to gain, yet Allenda gave me her undivided attention and she listened to my story word for word. She never judged or criticized me and I was taken aback by this. Most individuals ask fifty million questions as to the how's and the why nots, but she never did.

One evening I invited her to dinner because I wanted to know more about her journey and what happened for her to gain such deep insight into her purpose, I became intrigued with her story and after hearing more about her trials, tribulations, dark days, and the loss of loved ones I could do nothing but cry, I was in total amazement, and crying was something I didn't do. Expressing my emotions was very difficult for me because I chose to bury any type of emotional feelings that would connect me to my past and people. I believed this showed a sign of weakness and in order for me to survive life on the streets I could not demonstrate having any emotions otherwise I would be devoured by the evilness that lurked around every corner, you see the streets was my hustle and the streets raised me and taught me not to trust nor allow anyone into my circle, and I was determined to ensure that my sister and brothers could eat and have clothes on their backs and shoes on their feet. Living on the streets, life is very brutal and unapologetic and this is what I had become!

I marveled at how this woman has somehow turned every bad situation in her life into an engaging story that transcended into her journey and she has helped me to see how the things we experience in this event called life is all necessary. In order to understand your purpose and be able to stand in your faith you must become aware of The Necessity of All Things that we experience. As we finished dinner I shared with Allenda that I couldn't wait to get home to begin searching for spiritual and biblical information on how to begin understanding the meaning of faith and how to have a deeper spiritual relationship with the assimilation of self. During my drive home my thoughts became flooded with memories of a life long ago, things I had buried. I became anxious and wanted to get home quickly in order to get on my computer and begin searching the internet for books that would direct me on how to begin my journey with seeking out my purpose. Unknowing Allenda held the keys to my beginning she shared that she was in the process of finalizing her manuscript and I asked her what she had written and she shared how she discovered her Lifescript, the purpose of her living, and I immediately asked if she wouldn't mind if I read it. I jumped at this opportunity because I wanted to know more, I wanted to absorb as much as possible about her and how she evolved into having such a happy and purposeful life, and she didn't hesitate to say yes, and allow me the opportunity.

Once I received her manuscript I began searching through the pages hoping that I would stumble across that one thing or sentence, a paragraph that would grab my attention but something told me to stop and begin at the beginning. I was so accustomed to bypassing the unnecessary but this time I would need to start from the beginning. As I began to read I found myself falling deeper into every word I became immersed deeper into the manuscript it was if the words were speaking directly to me and so many questions began to populate my thoughts but the most important question I had was where do I start with my process so, I picked up the phone and called her and I asked her and she began to laugh and shared with me, at the beginning.

Allenda shared in order to begin seeking out any aspect of my purpose I had to go through a stage of dismantling each persona that I had created, this is a process of change and she explained that this would be a difficult and ugly process, she stated that everyone must go through this it's unavoidable and it's called **seeking self-discovery**, and this is how she explained it. "Seeking self-discovery requires going to God alone in prayer and fully exposing yourself, it will require being totally alone, no cell phone, television, or internet in order to begin healing you must speak every sin out loud that you've committed. You must confess every lie, every addiction, and every wrong deed and this is called, **acknowledging the demons**. The reason for acknowledging your demons is to allow yourself to hear what you've done and what it is in it's true form, you see when we sin it's done in secrecy hidden so no one will know and this begins the ugly process of lying, hiding, sneaking where no one can see you in your dark form this is where you give birth to your demons and you give power to sin.

The immoral act of transgression is where evil loves to trap you and commit you to becoming as ugly and dark as the demons. You give life and permission for these demons to embed themselves within you and then it begins to evolve within your spirit, then your soul and you move into a new residency which has now become darkness & sinful actions. Once your residency has been established with your demons you begin the process of falling deeper into the layer of self destruction, this is the realm that the demons begin to take over your thoughts and wipe out any right or logical thinking they will reside within you and grow. These demons will extend their roots deep within you and they will become so adhered to you that you will only begin to hear their logic and the language that they speak. They will deceive and trick you into believing that those whom you've hurt doesn't matter because it's all about your selfishness. Demons makes you feel invincible and gives you a euphoria feeling that you'll never get caught, that you aren't hurting anyone and the lie begins to lie to you and everything becomes disjointed, out of focus, and the one committing the sin sees the damage but they are under the influence of evil and your feelings become numb towards everything and they begin to believe their own lies while attempting to convince others.

In order to begin the process of **purging your demons** you must acknowledge them in order for their power to be diminished. In order to begin the process of recognizing your truth you must purge yourself and you must speak your sin out loud in order to release the power or strongholds over you and your Lifescript. Any sin that's committed must be brought forth and acknowledged, you must be honest with God because this is a test to determine your own self-awareness. I don't believe that most understand that God knows I truly believe that once a person is under the influence of sin they tell themselves that no one sees what their doing but fail to remember that all is seen and God knows. Once you've acknowledged your transgressions and after you have completed calling out your sin(acknowledging), now you must look at yourself and stand before a mirror and look at the person who committed each sin (transgression) this is called **revealing.**

You must acknowledge the Devil you know, you must look at the reflection of yourself in the mirror and see the person who committed the sin, before you can resurrect any true part of yourself, you have to understand that you gave the demons and evil persuasion permission to reside within you. You are the one that gave yourself away to darkness and it's not for certain how long you may have played in the devil's playground losing to this destructive game, wondering or dancing with the devil that you didn't know, but once you have found or discovered yourself you can begin the process of resurrecting the person that you lost but at a price. Every wrong action and or decision comes with consequences!

What you must understand is that these steps are important in order to begin to capture your truth. Speak your sin looking at your reflection because you must come to know how your life came into an evil realm and you must understand that you we're the cause of your life's direction and you must be accountable of how everything came about and began. This process is another difficult aspect of **seeking self-discovery**. Seeing yourself in it's true form can be a difficult and a brutal process, because most of us deny that we've committed any type of wrong doings or sinning, we even try to convince God that we haven't done anything wrong and it continues to grow and keeps us dwelled in being lost and in our own personal hell.

Sin takes control of every aspect of your life sinning is easy, the difficulty of life is living and following instructions, paying attention to what the Universe is saying to you, listening and seeking the message or gaining the lesson every single day. Facing your demons allows you the ability to stand in your truth and go before God and ask for strength and guidance. You must humble yourself and be pure and true with your intentions you must ask for God's forgiveness you must honor the Universe and be as a new person with a renewed mind and spirit.

After you have asked for forgiveness your spirit will require a rebaptism or for some a total baptism a rebirth, renewing, you can't begin living in your purpose unless this step is completed because the next most important aspect will be the process of removing all of the masks that you created from lies. These lies showed you a different way of living because of how the darkness lead and guided you into believing a perfect mistruth. This is needed because you've been consumed in an unhealthy dark environment of iniquity. In order to receive clarity and instruction you must reprogram your thought process so that it will be in accordance to your purpose. The Universe will align you with words of healing. Once the masks have been removed you will begin to see the world differently, you will begin to see the beauty in all things, and the ugliness in the wrong, you will now begin to respond to others in love, you will now begin to see life from the right versus the left perspective. God will begin to show you and unfold your purpose that was intended for you to live and then the beauty of your Lifescript will be revealed. You now have permission to begin living out that which was written for you, and you will begin to feel God flow through you". I was speechless after listening to how she took the initiative to begin a change within herself but unbeknownst to her this change would later come to assist others with giving them the encouragement and inspiration to begin their journey with understanding or becoming interested in recognizing their purpose. I was blown away and I thought to myself I needed this in my life so badly and I wanted to begin my own transformation. I knew it would be painful and extremely difficult but I wanted a change I wanted to begin feeling good about myself I longed for the day that I looked forward to waking up each morning. I was ready and wanted to face my demons. I no longer wanted to live in darkness where I had played and hid in the shadows. I was tired of living in a cesspool of mental darkness I wanted to love myself in my true form and love the person looking back at me in the mirror. I was afraid of discovering and knowing the truth, I did not want to face my past nor my demons but in order for me to have fulfillment with my life this was necessary in order for me to become the woman that God intended me to be.

As I came to realize what I had buried it blows my mind to know and understand what I invited and allowed into my spirit.

I allowed so many ugly and toxic things into my life, lies, deceit, sexual deviants and to think of all the wrong things I did to others caused me to grieve. As I began to dig deeper into my spirit I desperately wanted my true self to emerge and begin completing each step. As I went deeper into my subconsciousness it caused me to morun and feel the wrongs I had committed, it was a very difficult process and despite the fact that at times I didn't like the person I saw in my reflection I had to commit to the process. As I continued to bring forth my true self all I could think of was how Allenda was right there's no other way to begin and I shouldn't place a time limit on how I come into my truth. I must address each aspect of the ugliness within my spirit, and this can't be rushed. If this is rushed or not taken seriously God will let you know, God will not allow anyone to be fake or presumptuous, He will not allow a brazen person to play with the Universe, the Law of Creation and I didn't want to continue to fall under the spell of the ugliness of my previous life.

As I continued to confront each personae of myself I literally became ill, sick from the vail things that I had begun to remember I began to feel every sin that I had committed every single one of the transgressions that I had done came to revisit me and at a huge price my spirit! I began to see how I had compromised my soul! When I made the choice to live within darkness I never stopped to think if I had to pay the consequences for any of it. It is stated clearly that the wages of sin is death everyone will pay for their transgressions regardless of their requests for forgiveness there would be a price to pay for all of the wrong things I had done.

I remember hearing a minister on television speak about the ill-mortal sin of mockery and the consequences that yielded and for some reason this captured my attention and I became intrigued and I wanted more. The minister continued on with his sermon and he shared how the bible defines mockery as a betrayal against God's

Laws and if we are truly in faith we should always be careful not to walk, stand or keep company with those who scorn God because He will not tolerate anyone who mocks Him. I began to question myself, have I committed this sin, have I turned my back on God? I became overwhelmed with emotions because I believed that I had committed the ultimate sin on so many levels and I remember falling to my knees asking God's forgiveness, I begged and pleaded, I wanted my life right and once I was able to gain my composure and rise to my feet I decided that this would be the day that I would become a woman of integrity who stood in her truth.

I began calling around to local churches asking where to locate scriptures on forgiveness, love, and faithfulness because I wanted to understand more about it. I came across more scriptures that spoke about the Laws of how we should live and the knowledge we should seek and it seemed as if the words from the bible began speaking to me. I've come to understand how mockery is defined from a biblical perspective, I've come to learn that it may be easy to see the errors in others or with church goers but it is more difficult to recognize the spirit of mockery in ourselves. I see and hear how believers are so critical of others who mock God but not recognize their acts of mockery and what's most dangerous are the lies we tell ourself, and these lies begin to dwell in our own hearts. We become guilty of committing all types of sin and we don't see how our actions don't line up with our vow of faith. An outward show of spirituality or godliness without an inward change of heart mocks God. 2 Corinthians 13:5 "Blessed is the man who walks not in the counsel of the wicked, nor stands in the way of sinners, nor sits in the seat of scoffers; but his delight is in the law of the Lord and in His law he meditates day and night".

God knows the heart of every man and woman, He knows whose hearts are turned from Him we would do well to examine ourselves as to what is truly dwelling within our spirit. If we are truly in faith and then we need to be sure our actions are in alignment with the words that we speak. I will continue to grow and learn how to stand firmly in my truth, I will always remember to listen and look for the lessons and messages with everything that I do. Everyone should know and understand that the actions and words that we cast out will complete their cycle and grow into the thoughts that we created. We receive warnings, signs telling us to stop, do not proceed but we choose to ignore these messages and then the consequences begin. Eventually and inevitably mockers will be punished and knowing this it will keep me grounded and humble but most importantly I will continue to fall deeper in love with God and this will bring forth a deeper love of myself as I continue to grow in my spiritual walk.

I will always be a work in progress as God continues to shape and mold me, I will remain as argillaceous earth constantly being molded into the script written for me. I now pay attention to the whispers of instructions for my life. I will never be perfect I was born into the transgression of sin, therefore, I'm flawed and I will always be until I meet my expiration date. But for now I welcome each new day with love and laughter I feel alive and able to handle the events of life. I believe now my circle is stronger, I know my family and friends who love and support me. I'm wiser spiritually I can see and hear the things that will connect me into my purpose. I understand now why Allenda has a saying: "average is a stronghold, being great frees you"! The events of life will not seem fair or just; and at times you may feel that you are dealing with more than your share of heartache and pain, but you must keep in mind these moments are meant to shape you, you have to let go, walk away and trust the process.

Greatness is something that everyone should be in search of but in order to achieve this you must believe that you can do the impossible! "The Necessity of All Things" has opened my mind and spirit to the endless possibilities awaiting me. I'm honored to have met Allenda and this book has given me a foundation, a guide to follow that I can refer to when I need encouragement and uplifting. This book has helped me to bring about a change within myself. It's true what they say, if you let go and open yourself to the Universe and follow the signs, listen for the message, and learn from the mistakes your spirit will lead you into your purpose.

This events of life has so much promise of beauty, you will anxiously await every new day and fall deeper in love with living. This book is an excellent read from the introduction through to the last chapter. I knew I would be in for spiritual awakening an emotional connection and blessing and I have now begun the process of seeking a higher understanding of my purpose that was written long ago into my Lifescript.

It has been a rewarding experience reading this book it has changed my perception of how I view everything in my life on so many levels. I'm extremely proud of Allenda and I see nothing but success for her, she will not allow anything to get in her way and if it does it will not be in her path for long. This is the type of book you want to pass down to friends, and family, or for anyone in search of their spirituality or purpose.

"The Necessity of All Things", will always prove to be relevant and necessary in order to understand your destiny, path, direction or even better your Lifescript!
~Anonymously Honolulu, Hawaii 2018

Dedication

For my parents Mr. & Mrs. Allen Henry, for without your endless love, prayers, guidance, support, and encouragement, I would not have become the woman I am today. Thank you for instilling in me at a very early age the meaning of prayer, church & worship. You both have been my light in my darkness, and because of this I've been able to find my way through my darkest moments. Your selfless acts of love has demonstrated to me the importance of how unconditional love should be. You've established my foundation and released me into the world to experience life and I took with me your teachings that helped me to survive the realizes of the world. You've always told us that the world would be unapologetic, cold, and a brutal mistress, and she will try to rob you of everything until she has left you with nothing. The lessons were swift and hard but it has helped me to see the disciplines to everything that you've taught us. Every tear I cried, every hit I received was necessary in order for me to discover God's purpose for my life. I could never repay you for everything you have given me, but what I can give to you in return, is my love and my promise that I will forever honor my life and my womanhood as you raise me to do and continue to make you both proud every single or never giving up on me, even though I may have cause needless tears and heartache at times, you never stop praying, and you never gave up!

Momma, I know you miss Daddy everyday and your love for him continues to grow even though he is not with us, but I do know your love for him goes beyond the grave and it grows stronger even though he's gone. Daddy has transitioned from this life to another but I feel his presence among us everyday. Momma, I love you so much and I promised daddy that I would always make sure that no harm would ever come to you, I promised that I would protect you, I promised that I would ensure that you are never alone, I made a promise to daddy that I wouldn't let him down and I will always do what I must to see you smile. You are a remarkable woman with so much strength and courage and I now know where my strength and fight comes from. God has truly blessed me with a mother who possess a strong faith and love for God, thank you for your love and spiritual guidance, I will honor you always.

Daddy after you passed I whispered in your ear and promised to take care of the family and that I would make you proud, I hope I haven't disappointed you!

For my daughter Ariana and my son Derke, you both have been the heartbeat of my life and you both continue to amaze me. You have matured & grown into beautiful adults with a strong spiritual foundation and I couldn't be any prouder of you. God truly blessed me with the gift of being your mother, and it has been an absolute honor and pleasure to give you my love unconditionally, I'm so thankful that God placed enough trust in me to be chosen as your mom and allowed me the opportunity to enjoy his precious gifts. Never give up, keep reaching, reach as high as you can because the impossible is possible. When I look at you both I'm moved with much emotion to see God working in your lives, it fills me up with so much love to see your aspirations unfold before you, I'm inspired by you both, you have shown me every reason to never give up, you've encouraged me to never stop believing! I will always be your biggest cheerleader, cheering and supporting you every step of the way! Give life your damn best every single day and never let anyone prevent you from living your best life now! Be the example for others to follow because you have shown me every reason that the impossible is possible. I promise you that I will never give up my dreams, I will continue to show you that everything is possible if you just believe it with all your heart and never give up! Always love each other, always be there for one another and never allow anyone to penetrate your circle, and remember dreams will always come true!

For my sister Alisa Francine you have been my calm during my storms, you've been my best friend and confidant, you've given me so much strength when if believed I couldn't go on. You give of yourself so unselfishly and you never look for anything in return. Everytime I think of how blessed I am to have such an amazing sister it brings me to tears. I've watched you grow into your purpose, I've witnessed your strength, and I've witnessed how much you love the Lord. Your beauty radiates from within and that makes you a rare woman and spirit. Thank you for believing in me when I didn't, thank you for wiping my tears, thank you for being the positive force in my life. Words can't begin to express my love and admiration. Keep making your dreams a reality, you've been my example of how to love spirituality. I'm honored to have you as my sister, and I'm so blessed to be able to love you more everyday!

For my Aunt Thelma Blackmon & MaryLee Griggs Parker, without your continued love, support and encouragement I would have never known the impossible was possible. You both are two of the strongest women I know alive, your faith is unshakable, your love of God undeniable, and when I think of the definition of a virtuous woman the two of you would be the example.

You both are of everything that is good, moral, ethical and exemplary! Words can't begin to express my love for you both! Thank you for keeping me grounded in the word of God by living as an example, and thank you for loving, encouraging me, and believing in me every with every step I made.

xxiii

For my cousins Vona Lynette Blackmon, Timothy Renard Blackmon, Vincent Griggs, Don Griggs, Adelia Griggs, Ida Mae Griggs (d), Curtis Griggs, Jr., & my brother Michael James, and Cynthia James (d), we have endured great trials, tribulations & loses together and you all have continued to provide love and encouragement to me when I needed it most. During my weakness moments you made sure that I received the love needed to get me through. You've given me your smiles no matter the problem and this has meant so much to me. No one can ever take the place of family and each of you mean more than the world to me. We can choose our friends but we don't have any say in our family, and I'm so thankful, and honored to have been blessed with you all as my family. The distance will never matter because I will always carry your love with me, thank you for loving me, thank you for being there to catch my tears, but most importantly thank you for allowing me the honor & blessing of being a part of your lives.

For Asante, a man that entered my life without being aware of what the Universe had begun creating years ago that answered both of our prayers to the meaning of love. We were two spirits seeking to make a deep connection while exchanging energies that would grow into what was predestined. Neither of us knew that the Song of Solomon would be lived out through our bond to unite our souls always. Unbeknownst to us we would both become immersed into something that had been created upon our conception. The love that we have between us has been interwoven into our purpose.

We both have searched and failed, we both thought we found love with others but it wasn't what was meant to be and we had no idea that our destiny would forge and ignite a love and bond so strong that the Universe confirmed our joining in everything. You continue to dazzle me with your spirituality and authenticity of the man you've grown to be. You continue to be my strength and encouragement you've comforted me when the world and

xxiv

storms came for me, you've protected me and shielded me from harm but what you didn't know is that I had prayed for this long ago. Your love of family, marriage and truth compelled me to desire more of you but what you didn't realize is that my spiritual quest was preparing me how to love, comfort, support and encourage you when the winds of hurt, pain, discouragement and disappointment would come for you. As we continue our journey and quest for a deeper spirituality together my love will be guided to only grow deeper and my affection to become intertwined with your soul. Who knew that we would cross paths and join as one, my love is yours now and forever.

And finally to my grandchildren Aiyana Blessing, Geronimo & Trillien Jay, my angels! I can't begin to express how my heart burst with joy and love at the announcement of your birth. I never imagined that God would bless me twice over, I'm so very honored. To see your smiles and to hear your laughter is amazing, I love you both beyond measure. As I watch you both continue to grow I pray that God will always protect and guide your steps. Never allow anyone to tell you what you can't have or do, the world is yours all you have to do is believe it. Always believe in your dreams, believe in the impossible and also love and protect each other always. Your Grandmother loves you now and forever and I promise I will be with you every step, every tear, every pain, every let down and most importantly I will be there to pick you up when you fall. Never give up on your dreams, always seek to win! Keep God first and remember the impossible is possible, just believe it with every fiber of your spirit. I love you!

The Best Is Yet To Come...

Introduction

I often sit and reflect on my life in amazement thinking of all of the things that were necessary in order for me to be present, here in this very moment and it feels so good to realize that I now stand in my truth! The air that I breathe is necessary, the hurt and pain was necessary, the days of loneliness was necessary, my losses and failures were absolutely necessary, but I didn't come into my purpose until the day I lost my father.

All these years I was being prepared for the moment of evolving into my purpose. My father's passing was an awakening that caused me to examine myself and realize that I didn't like the reflection of the woman looking back. The woman the woman that I had became caused others to hurt, the woman I knew had told lies, the woman I saw in my reflection tried to cheat her way through living, the woman I saw had lied to God. I made the decision on this day this woman had to perish I needed to become a different creature, extricated from the waste of all of life's events. I knew it would be impossible to please God until the old persona had perished. The person that I knew had fallen under the direction of darkness and I didn't realize I had become the devil that I knew I had to get rid of this ugliness and banish it and allow this evil to become obscured forever and the only way to begin was to acknowledge the entry that began my spiral into a dark abyss that all started with my selfishness. I had to tear every layer of the personalities that I had created I had to recall my past because of the hurt that I caused to myself and others, it all had to be dragged out into the open and I needed to re-visit and examine my actions. Everything I believed to be right needed to be immersed into the spirit of my purpose. All the years of listening to the wrong voices going to church just to say that I went without truly seeking God's direction not understanding how meaningful prayer was trying to be an example to my children but not knowing how. When I think of how I gave too much of myself to the wrong relationships, why? What was the purpose of all of this?

The following night I remember having a dream but it felt and seemed as if I was awake but I couldn't move my eyes were open but I could only see straight ahead I couldn't speak. I saw a dark figure but I couldn't make out what it was all I remember was being frightened. I remember feeling the bed shake violently and tremble so badly that I began to beg for it to stop. I remember trying to cry out for help but I couldn't I felt myself trying to fight but I couldn't, I could not get free from myself. I became very emotional begging God to help me, "please Lord, please help me"! I began to see visions of my soul in hell I remember feeling my skin burning, I felt the presence of something evil laughing and mocking me. I noticed my burned arms and hands move in slow motion reaching out and up I heard myself praying pleading to God to forgive me, "please Lord, please give me another chance to live", and then out of nowhere I heard this very powerful voice begin to speak to me in a strong tone the voice was very soothing but yet calming. I immediately began to feel so much peace and comfort although the voice I heard was frightening I didn't feel afraid. This voice wasn't a familiar person, I couldn't recognize it but I knew it wasn't my father or any other person of familiarity but as this voice began speaking to me as I was burned I began to feel comforted I immediately didn't feel any pain.

I remember hearing this voice speak to me and I felt the power in the words being spoken to me, this voice asked how did

I allow my life to become so toxic and full of deadly words of destruction, why didn't I listen. I believe that this question was being asked of me to see if I would speak my truth, I felt it was a test I became afraid to answer. This voice spoke to me and told me that the ground that I chose to plant my seeds which were my dreams, hopes and fears weren't established on fertile ground, the voice told me that the soil I choose was dead land unable to yield anything of purpose and this terrified me. This voice continued to speak to me and said unless I begin to listen to the instructions that were given to me nothing good would come to my life. The ground that I decided to built upon would not produce anything worthy, nothing from this ground would be permitted to grow. This voice began to show me what I chose to build my foundation upon was land that would deteriorate anything placed in it. It would not withstand any of the storms that were being directed towards me. The structure of my house was fractured and frigid the voice began to tell me that I had nothing.

All of a sudden I began to see how I allowed my visions and dreams to become dim and gloomy all that I had built with my life was done in doubt, vagueness and ambiguity. I had built a house of nothing I didn't follow the blueprint, I had built something without following the instructions. I assembled my life based upon the views and directions of others, nothing was done based on the instruction of God.

I began seeing myself driving in some type of fog without any lights, without clarity and I saw a storm approaching I was headed directly for it unprepared. I tried to close my eyes but they wouldn't close, I didn't want to see what was going to happen and as I watched myself driving the voice commanded me to watch as my life was being played out like a movie. As I began driving I noticed I was driving recklessly and I couldn't control any aspect of the vehicle. I was driving into other lanes hitting other cars with passengers and children I began to scream and then it happened, I caused a fatality accident that took the lives of others. I was watching my life being played out in a car! I was devastated, as I drove by the carnage I saw and smelled death! How could I be so reckless with my actions it affected so many some that I knew and some I didn't know.

I noticed that my eyes were still covered with some type of skin and each time I tried to remove it, it kept coming back hindering my vision it couldn't be removed. Somehow I was able to see myself driving, needless to say, it was frightening. I saw how my decisions and choices had affected so many people around me and I never thought about how my choices could or would affect anyone. As I continued to drive I saw a house that appeared to be my own and as I turned to pull into the driveway I felt my foot being pushed down on the accelerator, I felt the power of the speed of the car and as much as I tried to stop the brakes did not work, I tried and tried I just couldn't stop. I attempted to turn in a different direction but I couldn't and as I got closer to my home I became frantic and screamed "Lord please help me"!

I crashed into the house and cause the entire structure to come down on me and just like that everything was destroyed! In just a few seconds everything that I identified as my home was gone what I thought I had built was now just a pile of rubble. It was all gone there was no foundation, the seeds that I had planted had been dug up and scattered I watched as they burned, there was no life nowhere in sight. I saw myself wondering only to exist from day to day. This voice showed me that each time I thought I had my life together it failed. I was shown how life was defeating me unapologetically hitting me hard, life began to hit me with such force that it caused this indescribable pain, pain that I've never felt and then all of a sudden it was as if this voice had instructed my body to move and sit up.

I was suddenly awakened from this dream that I believed actually happened and after seeing myself I decided I could not live this way! The residual pain that was left behind was a reminder that I needed to become a better human I needed my spirit to be erected into the blueprint that was designed and written for my life I needed to be different. It was time to burn the old and infuse new thoughts, new energy, but most importantly I needed my spirit to be baptised. The woman I saw in my reflection had to perish I needed to resurrect what had been buried for so long. The ugliness, the bitterness, all had to go away!

I began to acknowledge that life is a series of events based on our actions and reactions we all come face to face with multiple choices that will be used as the bricks that will pave our pathway. The funny thing about these events is that they will continue to appear and be used as event triggers. Event triggers will identify where we live emotionally and this will remind you of all the wrongs in your life. We choose to ignore these events and we make the decision to write the script better than what was originated and in order for me to become a new self it would require me to go before God naked. I had to be totally exposed in my true form. It would require God's forgiveness, it required my flesh to die and my spirit to be baptist and reborn. I needed God to breathe life back into my human form, I needed life spoken into my soul. I required spiritual nurturing, I required being attached to an umbilical cord to be fed like a junkie needing a fix. I humbly asked to be placed into seclusion away from everything and everyone in order for my mind, body and soul to be resurrected from the ashes of my past. I asked God to wrap me in his arms and whisper to me the Songs of Solomon, giving me instructions of love, showing me how love should be. I needed to understand the power of forgiveness, as it is written in Isaiah. I needed to understand how to have patience as

Job lived. I needed to become a virtuous woman as Ruth. I needed to be reborn!

I began to feel His strength being transferred into my soul and as He began to remold my mind and body I asked God to recite the book of Proverbs so that I would receive His instructions on living and loving in the spirit. As He continued to work on me I asked God to cradle me as an infant and read the book of Job on how to defeat negativity and show me how to live in my faith and truth as I faced the complexities of living. I asked God for a different rebirth and He heard my cry.

As I began to see the changes with myself God would continue to whisper His instructions to me, these whispers became the words that my foundation would be rebuilt upon my ground would become fertile and the new seeds that I planted would begin to grow love, forgiveness, understanding and kindness. As He continued to give me instructions it was explained that the final baptism of my spirit would require me to follow the instructions closely on each gift and these instructions would be infused into my spirit. I was instructed that I must not accept any ordinary love from any man. He shared with me that I'm only to acknowledge love from the man that He has forged through fire. He will be reborn a spirit ready to give you all of the desires of your heart. He will love you as Boaz with Ruth and honor you as Lydia who listened to Paul. This man will give you your dreams and more. He will have received my instructions on how to love you and you will know how to love him when he arrives. He'll bring a message to you that only you will know that was given by Me. You must come to understand that his love will be different, you must trust me.

I had awaken from my sleep I felt as if my soul had received a spiritual renewal and durability. I felt my spirit had been infused with the laws of Proverbs and the Song of Solomon. I began to understand the meaning of love and the reason for forgiveness. I felt as if I had been reborn and I would rise stronger than ever, I felt my mind was stronger and keener, my vision was clear and I could feel and hear every word but now with so much more meaning and understanding. God placed a new song in my soul and this gave me every reason to live life to the fullest. Everyday, I can now stand in my faith and truth that will allow me to help others in search of their purpose by being the example. I believed that I had been reborn from the lake of fire and my feet were planted on solid fertile ground. I'm now equipped to rise above and out of the negativity, I could see my way out of the poisonous fog that had been wandering through my thoughts, embedded in my mind and spirit. I thought I had my life together and on course, I thought to myself how could a 50 year old woman not realize that her life had become a byproduct of venom that brought forth bad decisions and wrong prayers. I knew my rebirth would require a lot of work and I knew it would be ugly so I began the process of tearing away each layer from my human body, my thoughts required purging, by spirit required a re-baptism, everything had to be torn away. My deconstruction would bring forth a tailored constructed stronger spirit as a new being. It would begin to awaken a life of love that would allow me to experience God's promises and this produced a deeper understanding of myself that caused me to fall in love with God more than ever.

In order to understand the meaning and or expression of loving yourself, you must understand that the unnecessary things in life are necessary. You can't get around bad decisions or wrong choices these are and will be necessary with living a purposeful life. The wrong and or bad relationships, marriages and even the people who call themselves friends, are all required during your journey remember everything is necessary.

The days and nights that I cried myself to sleep over matters that I believed to be unnecessary wasn't a waste. Everything that

I've experienced, storms, the good and dark days that I believed to be a mess with my life was all a part of a divine process that evolved into a beautifully orchestrated life and God was the conductor that set the tempo as He executed clear instructions that came together to be played according to the laws of life. The Creator had my life all planned out and as I reflect on my life I believe every event that happened was preparing me to embrace the teachings in order to understand the meaning of living and consequences. It's funny how the ugliness of my life became the greatest teachers that brought lessons of wisdom in the aftermath of every test. Each and every aspect of me matured into an example of how the principles of life's lessons can bring about a rebirth of a stronger better woman or it can become a consistent ass whooping until you get it, the choice is ours!

I've learned that problems or situations that one may experience shouldn't be locked away you never keep the ugliness in the dark locked up you must learn to release the past and the negativity. I've had to learn and practice the art of letting go. No one wants their insecurities and flaws to be revealed no one wants their weaknesses discovered, no one wants anyone to know that they've made mistakes, or made bad decisions. No one wants to disappoint their parents, or want their friends to know that they're going through difficult times and struggling to make ends meet. We must be willing to let go of the hurt, pain and disappointment and begin feeding life into your spirit. Learn to never hold on to things filled with frustration, discouragement, guilt and bitterness, you must begin feeding your mind with conquering the impossible. The impossible is the realm in which we should live, we should not be moved by the actions of others or things that we have no control. We must stop letting ourselves of the things we don't have or can't achieve, we limit ourselves with our words and actions, we must begin to change our patterns and begin living boldly, unapologetically.

We have permission to be free and limitless but if you refuse to let things go the ugliness, resentment and bitterness it will turn into toxic behaviors and this will and can turn into your prison and you will feed your spirit meals of poison. Before you know it, this will become harmful as well as hurtful to you and everyone around you, it will eventually destroy you. You must learn to release the things of life that serves you no good you must welcome and invite everything good into your spirit if not what you have planned won't yield the life meant for you, you can't rewrite a script that God has prepared for you.

You must be willing to learn to release all negative energy and begin living free in order to be elevated. You can't be free unless you release, once you've experienced true freedom it will be an unsurpassable high you will ever experience. Learn the art of release and begin to live free, never live with unbroken chains your life isn't meant to impress others, never live your life to make others happy. You can have the best life that has been scripted for you but you must understand that you may have to fight in order to reach your purpose. You must be more determined to let go of what's holding on to you. What's not meant for you can cause irreversible damage and you will lose out on the blessings that we're meant for you. The dark events in your life will be the moments of importance these events will produce the most profound lessons that will come to give you so much meaning. In order to grow it's essential to re-examine the source of toxic behaviors, schemes, games, circumstances and people, you must learn to trust the process. God does not need your help!

There will be times that we open ourselves up to the wrong people or situations, thereby, causing the voice of deception to creep in and we listen to the wrong whispers and murmurs that will then turn into dangerous actions of destruction. I've come to the realization that one of the most difficult disciplines in life is embracing change and in order for this to occur it will require letting go of toxic people and environments. You must cut ties with toxic influences, relationships, situations and circumstances. Whether it's family or friends it must happen in order to move forward. Your life has been built based on decisions and choices of good, bad, painful or sad, therefore, in order to have a life worth living, you must allow yourself to be guided, let go of the control allow the Universe to direct your journey because it will lead you into your purpose. The meaning of your life, every event you have experienced is the script that's intended for you.

Your script has been written but it can't unfold or evolve until you surrender and embrace your truth. You are on a journey, you will discover empowerment, love, and understanding and this will take you on a God promised adventure. Everything in life must complete its cycle in preparation for the divine process of what's to be; and at some point in your life you'll come to the realization that having a negative understanding of life will not get you to where you want to go. Your agenda will fail, no matter how much you attempt to go against God you will continue to be lost until something catastrophic happens to you. Running from your past or problems doesn't work it solves nothing, you must confront these demons at some point in your life cycle because the sooner you address the dark aspect of your life the better, why run when you can walk and lock each door behind you to ensure that the lessons from the past mistakes have been learned and every door of wrong choices can be transformed into a permanently locked door never to be opened again! Nature wants us to see how all things work together for the good of those who love life in pursuant of our purpose.

People expect change in others but never willing to change themselves. If I want to see change in others then I must be the change that I wish to see. If I want others to be better then I must be better. If I want my loved ones to change then I must be that change. If I want my children to become a certain way, I must live that way and be the example and not tell them how to be but be that person. If I want my children to be kind I must be kind. If I want my children to become a certain way I must live that way I must be that example. If I want my children to live fully as themselves and not wear any masks to fit in with others, I must be free of masks, I must be that person free from fear and free of judgement and live as I wish to live. If I want people to be giving then I must be giving, giving of my time, my love, my spirit, and my presence. Before I ask of any change I must first be that change!

The Universe has a plan for each of us, the script that has been written and so the journey begins. Everything will come full circle at some point in our lives. Sometimes, we get into the mindset that our plan is better than God's and we tend to deviate from the lifescript that gives directions for us to follow. However, no matter what our plans are, no matter what direction we choose, we will always be directed back into the divine written script for our lives. What people don't realize is that no matter how hard we try to rewrite, delete, or erase our mistakes, we must come to the realization that these events are all a part of the script that has been written.

Your story is the script and it will define your purpose, remember everything has been written and planned long before we were conceived, you must allow the process to be completed. You will gain a higher understanding of yourself but in order for your purpose to be revealed you must do the work, the Universe will always take over and the outcome will be far greater than what we think or have planned for ourselves. What we think or believe as being better will never yield or construct the same results as God's.

Our existence is based on "The Necessity Of All Things", but in order to discover your scripted purpose, you must understand everything that you've experienced will be and will always be necessary.

CHAPTER ONE

May 8th, 2012

May 8, 2012, 4 days until my 50th birthday, 4 days away from my Mediterranean cruise, let the countdown begin!

2:30pm My father was sent down to have an MRI due to the pain he was experiencing in his left arm, he said it wasn't bad but it had become annoying his arm was hurting and he asked if I could get the nurse. I immediately jumped up and went to the nurses' station and spoke with my father's assigned nurse and she stated she would be right in. I went back to the room and told my father that the nurse was coming. I asked my father to describe the pain and he said "I don't know how to describe it, but it hurts". I said ok the nurse should be in shortly, once the nurse came in she spoke with my father and asked him a few questions; "Mr. Henry where is your pain" and he responded "my left arm", he went on to say that his arm kept falling asleep at times and could he get something for pain. She proceeded to check his vitals and she stated everything appeared to be okay and that she would get him something for pain and that she would call the doctor. A few minutes went by and the nurse returned and shared with us that she had spoken with the doctor and he recommended that my father have an MRI to see what's going on. My mom and I agreed with the next steps and we felt some solace knowing that my father's physician was taking every step to determine the cause of his pain. I've worked in healthcare for over 30 years and I was trying to figure out what could be wrong!? Now, I'm not a doctor but I've witnessed patients have heart attacks, strokes, and other illnesses and I thought I could figure this out but who was I fooling, I'm not a freaking doctor I just wanted someone to give me and my mother an answer and take the pain from my father I wanted him to feel some level of relief. My father was fighting for his life and I wasn't going to leave his side since he began this journey and all I could do was to ask God for help.

3

My mom shared with me once they come to get my father for his test she wanted to go home to shower change and walk the dog, she said that she needed to get her hair done and that she shouldn't be that long and I said okay take your time I'll be here. The nurse came back in and said that she would give my father some medication for his pain before he goes to have his MRI procedure she wanted to be sure that my father would be comfortable during the test. A few minutes went by and the patient escort came to get my father to take him down to Radiology but I told them to wait a minute I needed to get the nurse first so that my father could receive his pain medication before they took him down. The nurse came and I gave my father a kiss on the forehead and told him everything was going to be okay and that I'd be here waiting for him. My mom kiss him and told my father she was going home to shower, change, walk the dog, and get her hair done and that she would be back as soon as she could and she would bring my father some soup to eat from one of their favorite restaurants. They both loved the broccoli cheese soup from this restaurant and my mom knew he would be looking forward to getting that spoon into that bowl.

As they prepared my father to be transported to Radiology I couldn't help but to watch their every move I didn't want my father to suffer any unnecessary pain or harm. I even watched the nurse administer my father's pain medication through his IV to ensure he had received enough so that he would not experience any further pain. My father noticed how intently I watched their every move he asked if I would be in the room when he got back and I said "yes sir", I'll be right here. I watched them roll my father down the hallway until I couldn't see him any longer and it felt as if I would never see him again but I quickly shook the thought of this away. I turned around and went back into my father's room and sat on the bench and I began watching television and from time to time I would walk to the doorway to watch the other patients and their families or I would walk over to the window and just lookout and stare into the sky with no thoughts. I wasn't thinking about anything no thoughts came to mind only a blank stare into a beautiful mid-afternoon sky. The television was on but I wasn't watching it the television was watching me. I wasn't paying any attention to it, just waiting for my father to get back I began to pace the floor wondering, analysing what could possibly be causing my father this pain. My father had gone through previous testing, EKG, chest X-ray, lab work, MRIs, CAT scans, chemotherapy, and radiation in such a short time and with each test the results yielded nothing, absolutely every test came back normal! Each test/ procedure that my father went through I would hold my breath and pray that everything would be alright. Oh my God! I can't begin to express the relief that we all felt once the physician shared that my father's test results were all good and this was the best news to receive, no negative findings after each test was a huge relief. Now, we just had to whether the storm and get through the news of this cancer. We truly believed my father would beat this, the odds were in his favor.

This all began sometime during the evening of Sunday, March 31st, 2012, I remember this day vividly as if it was yesterday. My father went to meet up with my uncle and his pool buddies and sometime during the evening something medically happened to my father. The morning of Monday, April 1st I got up to get dressed to ride my bike to my parents house I remember this morning being so beautiful. As I began riding my bike I thought to myself that this is a perfect day the sun was out, the weather was so nice, it was a beautiful spring morning. You could see the flowers beginning to bloom, the trees were budding and you could hear the birds singing as if they were welcoming spring after the winter. You could smell the grass being cut it was a beautiful day. The weather had begun to transition from winter to spring I began to think about spending more time enjoying the outdoors. I shared with my parents that I would start walking with them in the morning to get my workout in. My parents were the example of healthy eating and exercise my mother would always stress to my sister and I that we needed to begin getting our bodies in motion because the older you get the harder it is to lose weight or to maintain your health and she was right. Every morning my parents would walk 3 to 4 miles and this motivated me to begin exercising I would look forward to these walks because it was a time that I could decompress and bond with my parents. I remember pulling into my parents driveway parking my bike and walking through the door saying "Morning! Let's get to it, let's get this day started"! Depending upon the weather or my parents decision we would sometimes walk down Lee Road thru Cain Park up South Taylor and back home, or my father would drive down to Forest Hills Park and we would walk the Cleveland Heights side, over the bridge to the East Cleveland side. The East Cleveland side has this beautiful duck and geese pond and there would be so many geese that you had to watch your step because of the bird poo. I truly looked forward to these walks we had the BEST conversations about life, family, relationships, marriages, hopes and dreams, however, this morning would change my life as I once knew it.

As I entered into my parents house I remember walking into the kitchen and my dad was sitting in his favorite kitchen chair and my mom still had on her work clothes, I said "okay people let's go, chop, chop", and my mom turned around and said "Allenda your father can't see out of his right eye", I didn't really hear what she had shared and I said, "Huh"!?, my mom turned around again from the kitchen sink stopped washing the dishes and said that my father couldn't see anything out of his eye on the right side. I heard my mom say that my father couldn't see but to hear that he lost his peripheral vision in his right eye, I just couldn't comprehend

6

these words. She went on to say that she didn't know how in the world my father had drove home last night. My father played in a pool league and he would meet my uncle and his friends weekly on Sundays at the pool hall and they would shoot pool well into the night.

My father drove a small black pickup truck it was a standard five gear shift, this was my daughter's first car and she had gotten another vehicle and my father decided to keep the truck so he could pick up yard tools, flower beds, snow salt and other home DIY materials. My mother was amazed that my father was able to drive home, technically without any peripheral vision you shouldn't be able to drive you can't determine what's next to you on your right or left, needless to say you are literally driving blind. Without having any right side peripheral vision my father could have had a serious auto accident. Whenever my father drove his truck he would back into the driveway into the garage and we couldn't figure out how this was possible because on the left side of our house there's a deep huge ditch and if you turn the wheels to the car or truck the wrong way you would end up in trouble, you wouldn't be able to maneuver any vehicle out the only way out would be a tow service but he did it.

I remember after hearing my mom share what happened to my father I began to feel as if I was in a dream I could hear her and I couldn't produce any words, I just couldn't wrap my mind around what she just said. I was stunned and I couldn't get my mouth to move or produce any words, I couldn't say anything. I just couldn't wrap my thoughts around what my mother had just shared. My mother said "Allenda did you hear me"?, I heard her but I felt it wasn't real, she said "Allenda"!! did you hear me? "Yes", as I began to shake it off and I said "yes" once more and my father asked me what did I think it could be? I remember saying "you know daddy it could be anything, maybe you had what's called a TIA

(Transient Ischemic attack), that's what they call a mini-stroke, or it could be glaucoma, or maybe it could be a result of high blood pressure, but you know what we need to call the doctor and get you in as soon as possible so we can eliminate some things and not assume, but you know what daddy it's going to be okay, we'll get through it". My mom called our family physician and they referred my father to one of the world's top Neuro Ophthalmologist, there are only five in the country and this one came highly favored and recommended. My father's physician shared that typically it's extremely difficult getting an appointment with this physician on short notice, however, they would contact their office to see about getting my father in ASAP! Shortly after my mother received a call from the doctor's office the same day and my father was able to be seen the next day, man this was a huge relief! My mom and I felt some comfort in knowing that my father would be going to the doctor in the morning, I told my parents that I would go with them to this appointment. I arrived at my parents' home early the next day because I didn't want my mother to be alone and besides I enjoyed joking around with my father because he would tease all of us to make us laugh but this day was different not one word was said in the car. The radio seemed to play louder, there wasn't any laughter you could see everyone was in deep thoughts the anxiety and worry was thick as fog. As I pulled into the hospital I let my parents out in front of the main entrance. I had told my mother I would find them just go ahead, because I didn't know how many other patients would be ahead of them.

I parked the car and walked into the building and as I walked towards the elevator I remember seeing a young gentleman with his wife or girlfriend and she seemed to be so sad but the lady with him held his hand and said "baby don't worry it's going to be okay, she kissed and hugged him". I remember thinking I hope I have someone like that if my health becomes compromised, just to see the love with this couple made you feel good. We both got off the elevator on the same floor and we walked in the same direction. I noticed that they were still walking in the same direction as me and I remember saying I wonder if they're going to see the same doctor? As I walked up to the desk I looked to my left and notice so many people waiting to be seen as I gazed over the patients I saw my mom waved her hand to let me know where they were and I saw the couple that was on the elevator sitting down still holding hands. I'm not sure why I became so fixade with this couple maybe I was drawn into their connection because in the short time I observed them I felt the love between them and maybe God was preparing me for what lies ahead.

As I sat down I noticed the waiting room was quiet and normally most hospital or physician waiting rooms can be very noisy with different conversations or children crying running around to discover new things to get into. As we waited for my father to be seen my mom pulled out her word search puzzle my father was looking around and me I just couldn't stop thinking of all the things that could be medically wrong with my father. The wait seemed long but in essence it was only an hour. My father was called back and my mom and I went along with him I remember going into the exam room looking around at the new medical equipment they had to determine neurology conditions within the brain by looking through the optics I was impressed by the technology. My father sat in the examination chair in anticipation and then the door opened, it was the physician, I couldn't believe she was the doctor because she looked so young but she was the BEST in the field. She introduced herself and asked what had happened and my mom began to explain the events and afterwards the doctor shared what she believed it could be but without further testing it was all probable. She shared her professional opinion what my dad could have experienced i.e., possible glaucoma, or a stroke that probably resulted from high blood pressure, however, in order for her to determine any of these she would need to perform a medical examination. She began by explaining to my father what she was going to do and from there she could determine the next steps. She began by performing the basic eye exam, this involved looking through the funny eye glasses that were connected to a long arm it looked like something out of a Sci-Fi movie she turned the knobs and asked my father questions, "Mr. Henry tell me what you see, Mr. Henry can you see on your right, Mr. Henry could you see on your left", she then ask my father to read the eye chart. If you've ever had an eye exam or a driver's test this is the eye chart that the doctor will ask you to read from beginning with line 1 through 20 to determine your vision acuity. After she completed the exam she explained to my father that it appeared that he had a stroke, but to confirm this she would like for him to have an MRI today. I then asked if she could explain to my father the reason why that he couldn't drive my father and I went round and round about his driving and he did not want his autonomy taken away and he was very adamant that he would drive and I said "sorry no you won't", "I'll get you a bus pass", and we all began to laugh and this did my heart a lot of good. We left the doctor's office and began our drive to another hospital in order for my father to have the MRI that the doctor ordered. We all began to feel a sense of relief because we had confirmation that it was a stroke and we knew rehabilitation would be the next course of action including some medications. The mood was lighter we began to have conversations. My mother asked my father what would he like for dinner and my father felt a little better and I felt as if a boulder had been lifted off my back, thank you Jesus!

We arrived to the hospital, however, my father needed to be registered as an outpatient in order to receive his MRI and I assisted my dad with the registration process because I knew there would be a lot of questions, however, I noticed that my father was confused and he wasn't able to grasp what was being asked or explained so I said to myself that it was the residual effects from the stroke, but he'll be okay.

CHAPTER TWO

Transition into Transformation

We sat and waited for my father to be called for his MRI, my mother shared that she had called my Aunt and she was on the way to the hospital. Shortly after my aunt, entered through the door I was so happy to see her and I knew this would make my mom feel some relief or even better. My aunt stands about 5'3" and she's walks with strong confidence, she a woman who gives love so freely but she will be brutally honest with you if you ask for her opinion. When you see her you immediately know she wasn't a woman to be messed with, and you would know automatically know not to bring any drama to her. She has this incredible strength and faith and she will only speak positive words of encouragement and love. Her presence automatically made you feel better.

There were a few patients ahead of us so we had to wait a while before my father would go back. As we waited we all talked and laughed and I heard my Aunt say to my mother "It's going to be okay, God got control of this" and to hear my mother say "you are absolutely right, God's got this", did my heart good. My father was finally called back for his procedure and he got up took off his jacket and hat and said "okay I'll be back". Each time I watch my father walk away it felt as if a part of me was walking away with him my father looked tired & withered full of worry and I didn't know how to make it right or make him laugh. The father I knew was slipping away and I had no control of it. I watched my mother with my father and I could tell she was breaking on the inside but she kept it together for my father and the rest of us but I knew my mother was crying on the inside. My mother never left my father's side, if he needed water she was there to give it to him, if he need the television station changed she was there. As I continued to watch my beautiful mother smile and look so well put together I thought how much strength it took for her just to wake up and face the day of not knowing the end result of my father's fate. My mother stood so tall and yet remained stoic, at times she laughed when talking to family or visitors, but at times I could see the sorrow and worry. I began to feel something deep within telling me that I needed to prepare myself for the day that my mother would need me. I felt as if a voice was leading and guiding me to the right scriptures. When I attended church it was as if the Pastor's sermons would be speaking directly to me every Sunday. I kept asking and acknowledging God for understanding & clarification but God remained silent. I began having very vivid dreams of my father and grandmother these dreams felt so real, as if I had been up all night talking with them. This one particular dream that I will remember always occurred one week prior to my father's stroke. I remember feeling as if my grandmother and I had been dancing all night, I remember my legs were tired, my feet were sore and the laughter we shared made me feel so good

We laughed so hard that I woke up with a sore stomach but what I distinctly remember was the conversation. My grandmother began sharing with me that everything was going to be alright, she said "you know baby grandma hasn't been with you for very long but I've enjoyed every minute". I replied "Huh!? What do you mean you've enjoyed every minute of it"? She said "baby me and your daddy have to go, but I want you to know that everything will be alright, I need you to stay strong and know that we will be with you always". I replied, "What do you mean you and daddy need to go!? Daddy is right here with me"! She began to drift away, she was leaving me, she began to fade into a white mist. I remember running after her yelling out, I yelled so loud, "wait, grandma, wait please don't go, I need you, I need you here, please don't go, don't leave me, grandma I need you here to help me, I don't know what to do"! As she began to fade into this mist or fog I heard my father's voice and he said "Allenda, I need for you to be strong for your mother and sister, especially for Ariana and Derke". I turned the direction of where I thought his voice was coming from and out of nowhere he appeared, my father had a look of happiness that I'd never seen before he was so happy, happier than I've ever seen him. He continued to say to me "I'm done here and I am ready to go with your grandmother, but before I go I need for you to know that there will come a moment very soon that you will need to stand strong in your faith and truth and never ever worry about anything, trust in God always, He'll protect and help you always", and then just like that he was gone!

I was awoken abruptly, I remember feeling my calves and knees were so sore as if I had ran or danced all night. My knees felt as if I had been on them praying for hours I jumped up and ran downstairs to see if my father was still there and when my eyes locked with his it was as if he knew about the dream, he hesitated to speak but the next thing I heard him say was "what's the matter with you, running down those stairs like that"? My response was "sorry, I had a dream and it felt very real", my father asked "what did mama say to you"? I didn't have a response I was speechless because this took me for a surprise and I couldn't respond, I didn't share the details of my dream with him but he knew. He then stated, "well it was just a dream, only a dream". This dream would very soon come into fruition! What I didn't realize was that my father would soon transition from this life to another and my transformation was about to begin.

I watched my father walk with the Radiology Tech until they went through the door and as the door shut behind them, I remember feeling numb, I can't explain it but I just felt numb and empty then all of a sudden I felt cold it was the type of cold that's felt down in the core of your bones that caused you to shriver and I wasn't sure why. I'm not sure why I was paying attention to everything that was going on I was in tune with my emotions and I couldn't shake it so I just didn't say anything about it to anyone. As we waited, I decided to walk around the lobby area to just clear my mind and to hopefully shake this feeling. I just wanted to not think. I sat outside for a minute to release these overwhelming feelings I began to feel when I got outside I just looked up to the sky and I began to pray and I remember asking God, "what does all this mean? Lord, help me to understand, I don't know what to do! Afterwards, I decided to go back in because I didn't want anyone to worry and I headed back to the Radiology Department and as I entered and as soon as I sat down my father came out, the tech said he's finished and that the doctor would call with the results sometime this evening. My father gather his jacket and hat and I asked "are you okay", he looked at me and replied "yes sir I'm good, let's go". My mother grabbed her jacket and word puzzle book and my Aunt put her hat and coat on and said "everything will be alright, God got this". As we all walked out there was this weird silence not one word was spoken until we were in the car, then my father said "well that's it all we can do now is wait", not one word was said from my mother or me. My Aunt had driven to the hospital in her car and she said she would call once she arrive home to check on my father.

After arriving home, my mother began to prepare dinner and she asked if I would be staying for supper and I said no, I was going to go to my place and get some sleep but I'll be back in the morning but call me after you speak with the doctor about the MRI results. On my way back home not having any thoughts I did not have thinking on my mind, I don't even remember hearing the radio I just remember driving, I honestly don't remember driving. No sooner than I put the key in the door and crossed the thrush hole into my apartment, my phone rang, my heart began to beat rapidly, my stomach was in knots and as I look at the caller ID it was my parents number! I snatch the phone from the wall "hello"!! It was my mother and she said "Allenda, the doctor said the MRI confirmed that your father had a stroke and that she would need to get him scheduled for follow up care and that the doctor would be calling in a blood thinner to get your father started on". As I exhaled I replied "Thank you Jesus, Okay, now I can sleep" and my mother said "yes, now we all can sleep". This was a huge relief because we felt it was serious but nothing that we couldn't get through as a family.

The next morning I arrived at my parents, feeling so relieved, ready for the day and I knew my mother and father would be ready to go walking in light of the semi good news we had received yesterday. As I entered the house my father's back was to me and it seemed as if he had turned around in slow motion and I remember him saying to me "who are you"? I replied back "daddy stop playing, you know who I am", I thought my father was joking with me, because he would always kid and playing around just to make us laugh this was his way of making sure there was nothing to worry about. My father would always start my day, with laughter. He was the family's go to, to begin our day off good, he would call my sister and I every morning to make sure we were okay and if he missed talking to any of us in the morning, I could count on getting a phone call in the afternoon and he would always say, "what's going on, walk one talk one" and I knew everything would be alright, anyone he encountered he had a way of making them feel good and at ease, my father viewed life from a positive perspective everyday! My father wasn't a confrontational person he didn't like nor believed in drama he didn't believe in arguing it would bother him he use to say "why"??? "What's the point in being upset or mad it's such a waste and it never fixes anything". He would always tell me, "stop wasting your time arguing with people, it does no good. People will always challenge you with their words and there is no point in arguing with a fool to prove yourself right, just let it go"!

My attention was immediately directed towards my father's behavior, I began to notice how confused he appeared to be he couldn't determine the difference between his fork or spoon he paused and couldn't figure out the jelly from the salt shaker and as I began to speak my mother intercede and share that my father had walked the dog this morning and when he returned to the house he couldn't deactivate the alarm, he couldn't remember the code and the alarm went off. The alarm company dispatched the police, when they arrived, my father was very shakened, disoriented and confused he was struggling with giving the police officer the right information to verify that he was the homeowner, luckily my mom arrived and she was able to get things straightened out. Unknown to me my father couldn't focus or remember the daily things that he had done everyday and after listening to my mom I knew something was very, very wrong. I could hear it in my mom's voice she told me what had happened and I began to feel numb and I remember saying "okay what's going on"? I asked this question because I didn't want to accept that anything had occurred. The kitchen became so chaotic with voices flying over my father's head and this caused him to become very nervous and emotional he asked if we not talk all at once he couldn't get his thoughts together and this was causing a lot of stress for him, he was struggling trying to figure out what was going, you could see he was trying so hard to figure things out. So, in a calm voice I stated to my mother to call the doctor right away something wasn't right and she bolted for the phone. My father asked "what's wrong, what's going on"? My response to my father was nothing momma is going to call the doctor so we can make sure you are alright, and he replied "oh okay", I couldn't tell him my true feelings I didn't want to add anything to cause him to worry. He turned his attention back to his food as if nothing ever happened, however, he still wasn't aware of what was going on and I knew something serious had changed from yesterday because his confusion was worst.

It wasn't long after my mother spoke with the physician office that the phone rang it was literally less than five minutes. My mother and I jumped up and out of our chairs frantically towards the phone but my mom got to the phone first and the way my mother grabbed that phone I didn't dare say anything I didn't want to knock her down reaching for the phone so I hung back and waited nervously, and with each hmm and ummm I heard, my stomach turned upside down with anticipation. My eyes were fixated on my mother's lips, I hung onto every syllable, every word, and noun I even read her facial expression and I began to ask, what? what? What did he say? My mother said to me repeatedly, wait a minute, just wait, I can't hear what they are saying, go sit down, as I turned away to sit down, I couldn't help but laugh because I felt as if I were a child being told what to do, I wanted to know everything that was being said so I could be prepared for the outcome.

I continued to listen to my mother speak on the phone with the physician, looking at her mouth moved so I could grab every word being spoken as she informed him of what happened, then all of a sudden and I mean literally within seconds I remember my mom hanging up the phone very hurriedly and she said "let's go", we need to get your father to the Emergency Room right away, my mother hurried up the stairs to change and I believe my instincts kicked in as I began to speak to my father in my mind I had to remind myself to be very calm and not look frantic I did not want to upset my him. I looked at him very calmly said daddy we're going to take you to the Emergency Room so the doctors can check you out and be sure that everything is alright, my father looked at me and replied "okay". I'll never forget the look on his face he appeared to be so lost he looked so helpless I just wanted everything to be over and back to normal, I wanted my father back but God had a different plan and everything would be revealed in a matter of weeks.

We arrived to the hospital and as I began looking for a parking space in the Emergency Room parking lot I asked my father did he want me to let him out by the door and he said "no, I can walk". I parked the car and we all got out and I remember my mother holding my father's hand and I just lagged behind. As we approached the main entrance to the Emergency Room I noticed there were these bright yellow pillars in front of the entryway to prevent cars or trucks from driving directly into the facility, however, as we got closer I noticed my father wasn't moving to the right or left, he was walking directly into the pillars and as I began to shout out, "daddy"!!!! My mother grabbed him by the arm and pulled him to the left of her and asked in fright "did you see those pillars"? My father replied "no, what pillars", I knew then that something was gravely wrong.

We entered into the Emergency Room I told my mother that I would give the information to the front desk person so she could sit with my father I remember giving the nurse all of my father's information and within a matter of minutes no sooner than I sat down my father was called back into the triage area. My mother accompanied my father and I waited in the Emergency Room lobby. Shortly after my mother came to get me they had taken my father to a room. My mother asked me to call my aunt to tell her what happened and where we were. I immediately called my aunt and she said she would be on her way.

CHAPTER THREE

Death... the Ultimate Proof of Life

Webster defines "ultimate" as being or happening at the end of a process; final, and when I think of "ultimate" I'm reminded of how we all will pay the ultimate price of our choices that can sometimes lead us through the valley of death. I remember as a child my parents taught us the importance of prayer. We were taught a prayer to recite every night before going to sleep: "Now I lay me down to sleep, I pray the Lord my soul to keep, if I should die before I wake, I pray the Lord my soul to take". This prayer has remained within my spirit always I will still recite this prayer even today when I have no other words. These words still provide so much comfort, this prayer still brings me so much inner peace and comfort because I know I'm being protected, watched over as I slept. I knew I would be kept safe in God's arms during the night and knowing this gave me the feeling of security, it made me feel as if a warm blanket was being wrapped around me on a cold winter's night. If it's time for my soul to ascend, I pray Lord you will take me.

As I grew older my prayers became different, bolder, stronger and filled with tearful requests and pleads for help because of all the unhealed wounds that inflicted my life due to the complexities of my bad choices. As a child I was taught if you disobeyed God you would be punished, I've feared the consequences of this but didn't understand it. As I grew and matured I began to interpret biblical scriptures with the wrong mindset, I was reading without understanding. I would see how others would commit themselves to relationships and marriages but they didn't seem to honor what they promised. I witnessed so many wrong doings and it didn't appear that anyone suffered any consequences. I never saw anyone being punished so I began to live my life based on my own terms, I began to believe that you could make choices that were not in alignment with God's teachings and not get punished. Each transgression that I committed became bolder I began to feel that I didn't have to pay for bad behavior or the hurt that I may have inflicted on others. However, the day came that every wrong action that I had done, bad choices, decisions, and lies, would come to pay me a visit by way of that old thing called karma, it came for payment and the cost was immense! The things that I choose to do without any thoughts of consequences began to take everything in my life that I had worked so hard to obtain. I lost jobs, I lost every tangible thing I had come to cherish. I lost friendships, I lost cars, and lastly I lost my self respect, what I didn't realize was that death was always around the corner waiting patiently for me to make the ultimate mistake in order to swoop me up in its arms and end my life as I knew it.

I didn't believe consciously that I would get into any type of trouble from my decision and or choices, I knew I would be punished by my parents and their consequences would be a piece of cake. Getting my ass whooped by my parents was the only punishment I knew until I came to understand the wrath of God's punishment for breaking His law. I knew I would survive moral punishment, but what I feared the most was death! Death was something that I didn't understand I knew it was final, the ultimate end of life, period! There would be no coming back no do overs. As the lessons of death began to take those close to me whom I loved the thought of not seeing any of them would frighten me, and I didn't want to do anything that would cause death. As a child I've always feared death because of how horror movies and television would show the brutality of this process, how demons would possess your body and mind and this terrified me but I was drawn into these movies and I never understood why but I kept watching them taking myself through the process of being afraid.

I would sleep with my light on and I had to ensure that the closet door was closed, otherwise I wouldn't be able to sleep and the one thing that truly frighten me were clowns! To me clowns were the epitome of evil and I believed they were Satan's death squad coming to take your soul away. I began to believe that clowns would send demons or have your body possessed to take over your mind and control your body and I did not want demons to come to get me. I didn't understand death at all I knew this process was the ultimate price to pay for bad choices.

I began to learn that death wasn't anything to fear, death was part of the process of living or our cycle it wasn't about bad decisions or choices it's about our script in which God had written. We all have an expiration date, none of us know the hour, day or time that death will come but one thing is for sure we will all experience the process of dying. Death is the realm of the unknown no one has ever come back to tell anything about the other side many have claimed to have seen it via a bright light, angels or some type of shadows, however, no one knows what's behind the door of death.

As I continued to mature in my spiritual walk I now understand that death is the ultimate proof of life and what I mean by this is life is a cycle of events, there are seasons that will come without any work from us, and life will always find a way to reinvent itself, transform, procreate in order to continue the process of evolution and part of this cycle is death. Death is a guarantee process to living without this we all would cease to thrive, there would be no beauty in the world there would be nothing, just emptiness, and what good would life be without the process of rebirth and I didn't come to understand this until much later in my life.

In my adulthood I would find my prayers had turned into begging and pleading sessions with God to help me. I began to feel as if my prayers were not being answered I believed God was mad, angry with me for not listening or following His instruction. I thought I was being punished I felt abandoned, left alone with no one, yet what I didn't realize was that my character was being built, developed, my faith was being tested. What I didn't understand were the instructions, but then again how could I. I wasn't listening, I wasn't reading the word as I should and I didn't even believe in my own prayers. But God continued to ensure that I would survive the enemy, He wanted to equip me with all of the right spiritual tools in preparations for a great storm that was headed my direction. But in order to fight or withstand an attack by any sources you must have a good defense and God wanted me to be prepared, so He began to get my attention through my weaknesses and the one aspect of my life that was the weakest would be understanding death, the loss of loved ones. He knew this would be the first sector of my life that I would be attacked because of my lack of knowledge and understanding this fear kept me a prisoner, God needed to indoctrinate me towards having an understanding about death and the purpose for it. He had to allow disruption to take place in my life so that my dependency was directed towards Him and this caused me to have an unquinable thirst for seeking direction. Life isn't meant to be lived in fear. I developed a thirst and this caused me to seek and listen everyday for instruction, it caused me to search for understanding this thirst caused me to depend upon my prayers, this thirst caused me to have conversations with God on such a deep level. This thirst caused a disruption in my life that created a deep dependency upon God and this began my spiritual journey. This began a process of awakening of my hidden self, I was gaining strength, I began listening, paying attention to everything around me, I was able to see things I've never seen before and my trust became unwavering. Believe me God will get your attention one way or another and He truly captured mine but He knew I needed to undergo an intense mental and spiritual mentoring and guidance without it I wouldn't be able to endure the storms or defend myself in the midst of turbulence.

The Angel of Darkness was preparing a mighty storm, the darkness always equiqs his soldiers with all of the things that were done in shame, he equips his soldiers with our past transgressions, to knock us down defenseless, he knew exactly what would bring me down, he knew how to attack and each time the darkness came it seemed to gain more and more strength. It appeared the Angel of Darkness grew stronger in strength as his demons depleted me of mine. I was spiritually weak, broken and lost. Death came for my sister and then my grandfather during the earlier years of my life and I wasn't interested in reading the bible. Then I lost my grandmother, she was my everything the closest person to me besides my mother, I began to question God, why? It just seemed to keep coming, the death of my cousins, whom I was extremely close, I became confused. But then the day of my father's death yielded me into a different perspective, my purpose would now appear. My father's death transformed me into my spiritual transformation of my truth. I began to obtain clarity and direction, my vision was no longer clouded. I didn't feel as if I was in a fog, I could hear and understand the whys and why nots! I was on a different level of seeking understanding and direction. I would no longer say, I don't understand the reason, I began to trust the process. It's strange but yet amazing how God gives you what you need in order to understand, even with the death of babies and children as hurtful as this may be I began to have a deeper understanding of the why.

As I grew in my spirituality I began to understand that death is required in order for life to continue. I began to gain unimaginable mental clarity and strength, I no longer felt my life or spirit was lost. I started receiving God's instruction through my dreams, He trusted me with giving me the gift of receiving visions, I would have very clear precise dreams of people I knew and sometimes these people would be the cause of great hurt and pain but God protected me. He would show me the lies and mistrust and when I would ask the person about it they would slip deeper into their own darkness and continue to lie. He also blessed me with having the ability to foresee trouble, He would send warnings and messages to me and the strange thing about it I would share my dreams or visions with people and they would look at me as if I were crazy, they were unmoved, they didn't believe me and all along they would be the one the vision was warning me about.

I began to withdraw and not share what I believe God had shown me to anyone but God quickly got my attention and told me no, you will not withdraw. I would come to understand and acknowledge the message, my grandmother used to tell me, if God blesses you with the gift of visions never abuse it and always pay attention to what's being shared, if not you will lose this gift. For whatever reason God decided to bless me with the gift of discernment, He gave me the ability to see things and at first I didn't understand it but I began to see the things that I dreamt happened I became frightened, I didn't understand. So I went to God and prayed for wisdom and understanding and sure enough God began to give me understanding and I was able to interrupt my dreams with clarity.

I remember the day God decided to pay me a visit, He came directly to me by way of my dreams and what I've learned God will answer you but when we challenge Him, He will come directly to you and give you an answer. It's true what is said if you ask God for something you need to be sure you are ready to receive it, but most times we are capable of embracing brutal truths. He will allow things to begin to happen in your life to show you how wrong you've been and tell you how you haven't been following His instructions. God gave me an answer, and He showed me how my life would cease to exist if I continued in the direction I was going. He began to chastised me in such a loving way for not listening or paying attention. He shared with me that my prayers had been answered long ago but the reason why I couldn't receive an answer was due to the infection of noise from others that caused doubt and uncertainty to be planted within my spirit. I couldn't hear because I choose to listen to what others had to say. He began to share with me the story of Job and how he never gave up, as He told the story, His words began to sound of poetry the words He spoke began to sound like music. He spoke of Job so proudly and as I continued to listen, I began to feel myself swell up with emotions, the words began to overwhelm and penetrate my spirit. He bragged of how Job had lost absolutely everything and he never doubted or questioned Him as to the why's. This dream was so vivid, so real and very powerful, it felt as if I was standing in a brightly lit void listening to a strong soothing voice explain to me the whys of "death".

God continued feeding me, He wanted me to understand that death is necessary, dying is the process of re-creation and it is the necessity of all things. Without death we will fail to grow, life would no longer evolve, death is the ultimate proof that life is real and our choices will impact our ending and this is why we must embrace every single moment that's given to us, there aren't any do over's, you only have one shot at this thing called life and we need to live our best possible life now and be an inspiration to others.

I awoke from this dream different, the questions I had regarding death no longer existed I felt so much love and understanding. I believe that I now understood the process of why death must occur. Losing anyone whom we love will hurt, but we must not lose sight of why our loved ones were called back unto the Universe. From the time of conception we have an expiration date and there is nothing we can do to change it, it's inevitable, we will all lose someone we love and it will hurt but we must trust and believe in the process.

He shared that we are the only living creatures that He has given "free will" and it saddens Him to see how easily influenced we are. He went on to explain that life will come with challenges, fights, and conflicts and each time these spiritual tests come to challenge us we fail. These events that are chosen will require you to sign over your souls to the demons of drugs and alcohol that will require intense healing to be brought back into truth. Some choose to stay in a dream reality some just give up and the very sad truth to these decisions is that at some point in our lives we must face our truths. We must face the demons in our lives in order to move forward. Drugs and drinking only shortens our time in this realm these things destroys our human bodies in ways that's unpleasing to God and we're the ones that decide to just take ourselves out of this miserable way of living. I believe we all commit the act of suicide in some way or another based on our choices and when we do these things the Universe will let's us know but we chose to ignore the warning signs or messages of instruction from God.

CHAPTER FOUR

Transcendence of Love

I watched the nurses and physicians run into my father's room, it seemed as if everything began to slow down, my eyes were locked on my father, I watched as he began to fade and slip away from this life into another at the same time I began to hear God speak to me and tell me not to cry. He told me everything was going to be okay but I wanted to run and scream. A weird feeling began to come over me, I began to feel my spirit gain strength I didn't feel any sadness or sorrow I felt at peace and this peace began transforming my thoughts. It was as if I felt myself leaving, fading, going away, it felt as if someone was tugging on me, forcing me to be still but I felt my internal self begin to leave from my body, I began to feel dizzy but I didn't fall. I felt myself beginning to understand the whys. I began to see my life in a flash, I began to feel all the things wrong become right the aspects of my life that wasn't in place, I began to see everything put into the right order; the whispers that were silent became loud, so loud that my past and present began to intertwine together into words running through my mind that I never heard before and then I immediately began to focus on my mother, Omg! I need to be there for my mother she will need me, I didn't have to ask God for help because everything was coming together, I was able to connect the dots of my life. I had received instructions prior to my father's death. Right now I just needed to know how to navigate through the chaos. I needed to be quite so that my words would provide comfort but who was I fooling I had no idea as to what to do next.

I watched my father's body become lifeless and there was so much chaos around me that I couldn't think clearly, I couldn't speak there were no words but I continued to hear the whispers of my life they were coming alive and I began to feel these whispers from within saying don't worry, everything will be okay, I will give you strength as I have before, just trust me. I couldn't understand why my mind would allow these words to be produced, my

35

father was dying! I didn't even know what to do, what were the next steps how do I breathe, how will I stand up without falling back down? Lord?! What do I do? I saw the tears fall from my mother's face, I saw sorrow begin to consume her spirit, I saw the tears from my aunt's face, but I couldn't do anything. I felt as if I were in a movie but it was being played out right in front of me there was no pause button, I couldn't stop it. The nurses and physicians continued to attempt to bring life back into my father's human body, I began to see the peace come over my father's face. I noticed the sun went away and a thunderstorm rolled in I heard the nurses asking us all to talk to my father as they perform chest compressions. I saw the bag pumping air into my father's lung, it seemed as if they continued to resuscitate my father for a long time but in reality it had only been five (5) minutes. I was at the end of the bed, my mother was to my father's right and my Aunt was on his left. I remember shouting out to my father "daddy, please, please DON'T LEAVE ME", I heard my mother ask my father to come back, I heard my Aunt say to my father "come on we need you, come back". The nurse check for a pulse and she said, "I got a pulse"! When I heard this I thank God for hearing my cry! They began searching for a vein to start an IV I heard the nurse shout out, we're losing him again! All of a sudden the room became full with more physicians and nurses they ask us again to begin talking to my father, they began chest compressions again. I began yelling at the nurses, "Oh my God what's going on, I thought you said you had a pulse, you said you got him back, what's going on"???? I felt my feet begin to move backwards, I felt myself become numb, I needed some space, I couldn't breathe! I felt my feet begin to move I remember taking steps, I wasn't sure the direction but I ended up into the hallway. I remember feeling as if I was watching a movie I saw the nurse goes into the room and asked my mother to step out, I didn't understand why or for what reason, all I knew was that I didn't want my mother to leave my father. I turned to my left and I saw my cousin walking down the hallway and I began to run towards him, he abruptly stopped, he had this look on his face as if he knew, he began to say "no, no, no, Linda no"! We held each other so tight, we both began to cry and all of sudden my cousin released me and said "I need to see him, this can't be true, I know Uncle Brother isn't dead! I began to walk back towards my father's room and by this time my mother had went back into the room, I didn't go back in because I just didn't want to deal with all of the chaos, I needed to wrap my mind around all of the events that were taking place. I just couldn't think! My mother began walking towards me and I remember thinking why? But as she got closer I began to hear God's instructions, I became nervous and I didn't understand anything that was running through my mind. My mother gently pulled on my arm and took me down the hallway and quietly explained that the nurse called her out of the room to explain that she had spoken with my father's doctor, and I heard my mother say the nurse just spoke with the doctor and he said to stop the resuscitation, it's been too long and the quality of life for your father is diminishing. The longer they continue the less the quality of life. As much as I didn't want to hear this, I said "okay" momma, they can't stop". My mother grabbed me and began hugging me and I knew it was time that I not be selfish, I had to let my father go.

I watched my mother walk over to the nurse and I listened to the words of instruction from my mother informing the nurses and physicians to stop performing CPR, I began to watch my father begin to complete his transition from this life and enter into the next, I knew deep in my heart it was over! My father's script had been lived and completed I would no longer hear my father say I love you, there would be no more you can do it, there would be no more fussing, no more sorrow, no more pain, my father had completed his life cycle, his purpose had been lived, his Lifescript had been followed according to how God had it all written.

I began watching the nurses begin to prepare my father's body for the funeral home and our family to say their goodbyes I noticed the room being immersed with so much sorrow, there were no words only silence I had no feelings, there wasn't anything to do, no conversations, or laughter, but what I knew what I had to do next. My next actions came with no hesitancy but then I thought I had to call my she had just left for Houston and everything was okay, she had just spoke to our father earlier this morning and I didn't know what to say or how to say it all I remember is staring at my phone and dredding dialing my sister's number. As the phone rang I remember staring out the window with no words I was numb and I didn't know what to say to her when she answers the phone. I dialed the number and hit send, I listened to the phone began to ring, one ring, then the second and then she answered I don't remember my words or much of anything but what I do remember is hearing is my sister cry uncontrollably I felt helpless, I didn't have any words to comfort her, there was no one there to hug her and then she said I'm on my way. The next call was to my brother and then my son, omg...what do I say, how do I tell him, he had just left yesterday. He left his grandfather alive, they laughed, cried and hugged and now I have to tell my son his grandfather was gone! I don't know how to tell him I just don't have the words, I remember my son saying, "he's gone isn't he", and all I could say was "yes", I listened to him break down in tears there were no words exchanged between us only tears and I remember my son saying to me, "Papa is at peace and I want to remember him when I last saw him", and I remember responding back, "okay, I understand", my father was my son's hero. The next call was to my brother and then my Aunt and as I continued to place calls, I knew

I had to brace myself for the sorrow and grief to come especially from my daughter, I had no idea what to do.

When my daughter arrived to the hospital and entered the room I will never forget the look on her face, and I saw her fell to her knees and as she began to cry, no one knew what to do or what to say, my family knew that my daughter was extremely close to my father, he was her everything and no one was prepared for this day all I knew was that my father's love would transcend and become a part of us all!

CHAPTER FIVE

I'll See You Again

We began to gather my father's belongings from his hospital room and as my family and I walked towards the elevators I had this overwhelming feeling tugging at me not to go I didn't want to leave my father behind I wanted to turn around and get him but I knew he wouldn't be coming. We all walked out of the elevator and as we walked towards the parking lot there was only tears and silence we all hugged each other and nothing more was said we all went in different directions towards our vehicles, and we all left.

The drive home was the most surreal moment of my life knowing that my father would never ride in the car with me or my mother again this was pretty difficult to accept, I had to begin thinking of life without my father. I believe my mother and I were numb and to see how spiritually broken my mother had become, broke my heart. As I looked over to mother I notice that everything had began to settle into my mother's spirit and at that moment God said to me "do not weep, do not be sad Allenda, your father is at peace, I need you to focus on helping your mother in every way", and after hearing this I immediately felt that everything would be alright. My mother said to me "Allenda, I'm going to need your help, we have to begin making funeral arrangements for your father", and I just didn't know how to process hearing this but I knew I had to I never thought about the day of planning my father's funeral.

We arrived home and I sat down I believe the events of the day started to catch up with me I began to replay my childhood when I was eight years old, when I would run and jump into my father's arms as he came home from work, I began to replay my teenage years remembering how my sister and I use to prepare my father's lunch for work and leave notes in his lunch box telling him to have a good day. I began to replay the day I shared with my father that I would be entering the military, and he said, "you don't have to do

43

this", I replayed the day my father taught me how to drive a stick shift and how he yelled at me because I would ride the clutch. I began to replay the day I went into labor and how my father ensure that I got to the hospital in record time, I remembered how he shared with me how beautiful his granddaughter was the moment he laid eyes on her, I began to replay the day I got married and my father saying to me before he walked me down the aisle "are you sure you want to do this"? I began to replay the day I called my father to shared with him the numerous college offers that my son received to play football and to hear my father say "and I will be front and center watching", I will always remember the priceless joy these words brought to my son.

As I continued to reflect on these memories, I remembered my father sharing with me how beautiful my daughter looked as she went off to prom. But what I will remember the most is how my father would be there to catch me after each mistake, he would be the one who would dry my tears away, my father was the one who told me after each wrong decision "to get up off my ass and do something about it", and I could count on him saying to me every single day how much he loved me and how proud he was no matter the mistakes or wrong choices and these memories lead me to write my final goodbye to my father that I read at his funeral:

May 8th, 2012, This Isn't Goodbye Daddy I will see you again...

"Daddy words can't begin to describe what I'm feeling right now, had I known that I wouldn't see you again I would have hugged you tighter and told you just how much I will miss you, but I assumed that I had more time & days. A big part of me die with you, there is now a hole dwelling within me and I pray that God will send me comfort throughout all of this. I won't say goodbye but for right now what I will say is how proud I am that

God blessed me with having an incredible father as you! You met and married a beautiful woman 50 years ago and built a strong family according to God's values, I just hope and pray that God will send me a mate to have in my life as you did. Daddy you raised us, to become the women that we are today, and you taught us how to handle life and tough situations, but what I wasn't prepared for was the day that I would lose you. You taught us that there would be days filled with pain, but you also showed us how to give it to God and never look back, you taught us that those same days could be filled with great joy and beauty if we only trust and believed in God. You taught us how to love unconditionally as well as how to forgive and move on, and these were the principles that guided your life based on God's terms and you did it unapologetically and without any complaints. I've made so many mistakes and bad decisions, but you taught me how to get up, shake it off and do it again and never give up! You have given so much and never asked for anything in return, I wish I could have given you so much more. Your style and impeccable taste and eloquence taught me how the world should see me no matter what, I can only pray that I will continue on with your legacy and make you proud.

You believed in family, you taught us how to love one another without causing pain. You believed in placing a smile on all of our faces in time of need and pain, you blessed us with the gift of laughter when you didn't even realize we were in so much pain. God snatched you suddenly because He did not want you to suffer. You fought as hard as you could but God had a different plan. I never once questioned God I told Him that I understand. As I think back of how God orchestrated every step leading to this I think of how we all have been so blessed to have you in our lives. For as much as I wanted to be selfish and keep you here, God showed me he needed you more. I'm trying to understand and take comfort from these words: "For God greatly loved and dearly prized the world that He even gave up His only begotten Son, so that whoever believes in, trust in, clings to, relies on Him shall not perish, they will not be lost but have eternal everlasting life" (John 3:16), and these words will give me the strength and comfort I need to move on.

Daddy I will miss our morning calls and conversations, I will miss our morning walks, I will miss your laughter and smile, I will miss you so much but I want you to know that my life has changed forever, I will never be the same. I know God has a message in this somewhere for me, I just need to be quiet and still long enough in order to hear and see what He has intended for me. I will hurt from this, but I will learn from this, but most importantly Daddy I will lean on and trust God even harder now. I know this isn't goodbye because I will see you again someday and when I do we can sit and talk about how you watched us all from above and how proud you were of how we continued on with your legacy. I love you Daddy and I believe you knew just how much"!

My father's death had been woven into every fiber of my DNA and spirit, his death transformed me into a woman that was about to be in alignment with living in faith and truth, the teachings and lessons of God would begin to transform my life. I would become a woman of integrity, a woman of impeccable words towards a higher understanding of how everything is necessary towards my purpose. From the moment of conception this event was stitched into the lining of my life script and it would be lived out according to God's divine will and purpose. What I've come to realize is that it doesn't matter what path or direction I choose to take, my father's love will always be within my spirit, my life would now become about my purpose!

I struggled with writing and sharing my story but I hope this will inspire or encourage someone, anyone to seek out understanding their purpose. I want to share the whispers of my journey in hopes that it will bring someone closer to God to see the beauty in how the Universe speaks to us everyday. Pay attention to the whispers that we all receive everyday and if we don't pay attention and watch for the signs and listen for instructions to the steps or direction it will come at a price.

Whether it's a warning, a lesson, or sometimes both we must understand what our lifescript is order to obtain our purpose. We must listen for the message or see what God has intended for you in life we have to understand the meaning of the little whispers or voices that we all receive while living in the valley or up high on a mountain.

After a conversation with my daughter whether I should or shouldn't write my story I decided to hold my breath and just do it! It took the words of my daughter that became whispers that I shall cherish the rest of my life... she shared "it didn't come too late; it came when it was suppose to whether you wanted it or not it's here"! There is a process and purpose to everything that happens to us and I wanted my story of my journey to be of help to the young, the old or anyone who may be struggling with their choices or decisions and finding it difficult to hear God while going through great pain and suffering, sometimes not understanding what God's purpose is for your life can place you in a dance rehearsal with the devil and we don't get it until it's time to pay for the dance and sometimes it's too late and we continue to miss out on the whisperings that God has intended for us because we are either too selfish or our vision becomes clouded in order to see the road. Take heed to the warnings and learn from them because if you decide to dance with the devil, He will take the lead and you will have no choice but to finish the dance.

CHAPTER SIX

The Caterpillar Knows

The caterpillar is one of the most amazing insects that God has created, it knows when it's time to begin the process of change, it never questions, or doubts why it's necessary. The caterpillar is defenseless born without any means of protecting itself from the evils that waits, after its entry into the world, but this doesn't stop the caterpillar from moving forward to gain its wings. From the moment of their conception to their birth the caterpillar understands their purpose, however, as humans we don't capture our understanding of our purpose until much later in our lives. The caterpillar appears to move very slowly from leaf to leaf and through the grass, but they move regardless of the fear. They don't run nor hurry they just stay the course towards preparing themselves for the process of change. The caterpillar has many challenges to face as they begin their journey but they never stop nor give up in spite of the obstacles. The life expectancy of the caterpillar is short and most don't realize the importance of this tiny creature but their purpose is so relevant to our survival. Once the caterpillar completes the process of metamorphosis within the cocoon it will emerge and take flight, the caterpillar completely transforms into a beautiful butterfly and begin the pursuit of their purpose, it's ingrained in their DNA, the caterpillar knows their purpose despite their short lifespan.

We make a decision to take the path of least resistance or the road of destruction versus the road of instruction, the destruction begins the process of building our character, destruction will guide us towards the intended script eventually, and the deconstruction would be considered the human cocoon that we enter in order to transition into our transformation of understanding how everything has been necessary in order for our lives to be unobscured. We could learn so much from the insect and animal kingdom, they are wired to understand their purpose, they will never deviate from the instruction that's ingrained within their DNA, and this is carried throughout each generation as their life continues to transition and transform over and over again.

My father's death ultimately lead me to the one thing I had been in search of and that was my purpose! I didn't always have a strong faith, I believed in God but I was just going through the motions. I was told by my grandparents and parents to always pray and seek direction from God, because if I did this it could change things but I didn't believe in my own prayers. I would pray to God and ask Him to show me my purpose but I couldn't see nor hear the answer because of the darkness I chose to listen to, I thought I never received an answer but it has been there all along. I couldn't hear the voice nor the whispers from God because I choose to allow the wind of confusion to disrupt my thoughts.

Life is about developing a subtle mind which brings about peace, calmness, love and kindness, a subtle mind allows you to remove the unnecessary chatter and noise so that you can move forward in tandem with what the Universe has to say to you. We must be still and quite long enough in order to discern and recognize the road ahead. We all have a voice in our heads that no one else can hear, this voice we often choose to ignore most of the time. This is what guides and directs us with the events in our lives and the choices we make. But in order to hear and receive what's being said we must quiet the noise and discipline ourselves to be still long enough to pay attention.

Understanding how to reach within and see others from a loving perspective and not judge or criticize them for their choices or decisions can sometimes cause us frustration. Sometimes we can view individuals from a bias stance and share words of hurt and pain without placing their feelings into consideration. But if you aren't careful deception will begin to infiltrate your spirit while asking God over and over again for an answer and we become blind to our own foolishness. As I waited for God I couldn't see my way because my vision was clouded, my thoughts were polluted with listening to advice from people I thought had my best interest, I didn't understand, I was confused and so lost. I drifted in the fog for so many years. I did not believe in what I was praying, I was in a place of deep darkness while living in a valley, the feelings and emotions I experienced were terrifying. I was making choices based on what look good on the outside and then discovering it wasn't and I was becoming uglier by the minute. I needed help and the day my father died that help came, my father's transition catapulted me into my transformation. I remembered how everything appeared to move in slow motion but everything around me became so clear, I finally began to see the road, the direction & journey that was intended for me became so real. It was always there but I just couldn't see it, I ignored it, I ran from it, I excused it and hid, but what I didn't realized nor understood was that you couldn't run from God, He found me every time, He never left me, I left Him! I remember this day so vividly, this was the day that I totally released and surrendered to God. I cried uncontrollably the tears just didn't seem to stop I asked God to please forgive me for not listening, I asked to be forgiven for ever doubting Him, this was the day I truly experienced humility, this was the day that I began to understand the power of letting go! As crazy as this may sound I felt so alive, this was the day that I realized how everything was necessary for me to be right in the moment and feel every breath I inhale, I had created peace within myself, and I began to invite the gift of love into my spirit. The love for God has been the greatest love story and I'm enjoying the romance that has begun between us. It took me fifty years to begin to see things in their true perspective, I'm able to hear many things through the noise, because now the noise has become music to my soul.

In order to discover inner peace and have the romance of your life with God you must reach deep from within and pull back the layers of every persona that you created and acknowledge your demons. Change is and can be painful but this process must take place in order for the Universe to begin the process of opening up the beauty in all things. Life must always be perceived from love and not from a place of negativity because this can bring about a lifelong cycle of bitterness and unwanted feelings and emotions that will prepare you for a long dance with the devil and his demons.

We are all reflections of previous people and moments of our past and how we integrate or merge these subtle personalities into our spirit that will create the journeys of a script not written by God, but these are the moldings that create the events with our lives.

The lessons and experiences has helped me to push through and I refused to acknowledge failure. You see being down in a valley my demons would chase me unrelentlessly and it began to feel as if my life was a 24/7 hide and seek game but looking back I see how these events molded and pushed me throughout my life.

My cries for help I believed fell on deaf ears, I didn't think anyone was listening I felt alone and lost. Every decision I made was placed on a collision course my decisions and choices weren't being guided, my decisions were based on selfishness and wrong desires. My prayers did not consist of love and forgiveness, I prayed for revenge, I prayed for the suffering of those who hurt me, and because my prayers were based on selfishness, God allowed my decisions to show me what happens when we're self centered and poisoned with wrong thoughts.

During this season of my life I was filled with so much bitterness, hurt and pain that it turned into destructive behavior and thoughts and this began to run very deep within my spirit it began to turn my outward persona into this ugly, angered woman. I allowed the hurt from others to consume me, I allowed every negative word that was said to me to penetrate my spirit I allowed the negative energy from others to begin to affect me and from this I became a very unpleasant person. I had created a persona that evolved into cutting you down with my words and I did not think twice about your feelings. I became a persona that no longer cared about anyone's feelings it became a game of how bad I could hurt you before you would even think about hurting me. This became my payback to those I felt deserving of my wrath or anyone who I wouldn't think twice about hurting. I became so bitter that my feelings developed into this impenetrable fortress that did not allow anyone into my space or world.

I had become so disinterested in relationships and I never allowed any connection with men to go beyond or last longer than 90 days and this became my rule with anyone. I didn't care how much a man would tell me he "loved" me, love meant absolutely nothing love had become a joke and I was only going through the motions. I became so disgusted with the games that people played and I refused to be a part of this mess any longer this was my way of fighting back! I was so disengaged from having emotions or feelings I wasn't interested in creating any bonds with anyone. I just wanted to be alone because I felt this would keep me safe from harm, I believe I didn't need anyone but this bitterness had gotten so out of control that it was beginning to affect my relationships with my friends and family. I remember my father used to tell me that my attitude was terrible and that I needed to check myself, he used to say to me religiously "don't nobody want to be around someone with a nasty attitude, no one will ever see your beauty because of your this, you're so set on keeping people away from you" and I would reply by saying "good that's just the way I want it". I didn't realize that the person that I had created began to lash out towards my family and I couldn't control this person any longer the ugliness had become so embedded within me, she was my protector and I had become comfortable with my altered ego taking the lead because this made me feel invincible but what I didn't realize, was that now my family didn't want to be bothered with this ego I had created and I didn't know what to do.

I remember going to God to talk to him as if I was talking to my parents, or a friend. I didn't know how to begin so I just started out with telling God how pissed I was with how people hurt me and it didn't seem as if they were being punished for their wrong behavior. As I continued talking to Him I just let it all go, I released my hurt and pain to Him which was something I had never done before. I remember begging God to fix me I remember asking God to help me! And unbeknownst to me He would answered loud and clear!

Sunday, October 31st, 2010, I remember this particular Sunday that I attended church and the sermon was about "How to Handle Things", and this got my attention immediately, it was as if God moved my head to look forward and cleared my thoughts so that I could absorb every word that was about to be spoken, and I know everyone can related to this feeling because it was like the sermon was written specifically for me. As he began to preach, he gave an introduction into the sermon "without the Lord indwelling you, without Him interceding for you, without Him instrucing you and without Him inspiring and encouraging you, you cannot handle things"! Okay, now I knew God was speaking directly to me, the Holy Spirit was about to perform a spiritual baptism with my spirit. Before the sermon began I began to feel emotionally overwhelmed, I began to revisit how this ugly persona I created came into fruition, I began to revisit the hurtful words that were spoken to me by people whom I thought loved me, I began to feel the hurt all over again, but this time it was different. I remember holding my head down in shame and as I revisited how I spoke to people, I began to feel the words I had delivered, and as each tear fell, I repeatedly asked God to forgive me.

God began to speak, He shared that there were three steps on how to handle the events of life: (1) Prepare yourself for things, trouble is promised, John 16:33 & Timothy 3:12; deliverance and joy is also promised, Psalm 34:17 & Psalm 30:5, be ready to handle both, Philippians 4:12-13. (2) Push things out and away from your heart and mind with God's Promises, Genesis 42:36, things of lack cause panic, push them out and away, Philippians 4:19, Psalm 37:25, things of loss cause grief, push them out and way, Isaiah 61:3, things of eeriness cause fear push them out and away, Philippians 4:6-7, purging things out and away with the promises of God will root and ground you in the will of God and then things cannot move you, Proverbs 19:21. (3) Plant yourself in the things of God, Acts 20:24, plant yourself in his call to conquer things, Romans 8:37, plant yourself in his command that prospers in things, Isaiah 55:11, plant yourself in His comfort in the midst of things, Hebrews 13:6. Everything that is against you is for you, Proverbs 16:4! This sermon was the beginning of the deconstruction of an altered persona, an ego that was created out of pain and hurt, this ego would be buried in a tomb surrounded by the scriptures written by God and she will never be resurrected again. I knew this would be a process but I hadden taken the first step as God called me to take on October 31st, 2010.

We begin our life in the womb, we live our lives innocently as children, we begin to live and view life as young adults and as we continue to grow older we begin to experience the hardships and struggles somewhere in the fog and we get lost. During these times somewhere between the hurt and pain it starts to penetrate your spirit shifting you from one mental extreme to another and before you know it, you can't find your way. So where and when do we begin to live? You don't and won't until the mess you created becomes what is meant to be. I didn't begin to live and see the beauty of my life until the age of 50. It was there all along but I was too reckless to see it, I wasn't able to appreciate my gift, I was discovering when you create your own path and follow different instructions without God you get lost.

I had received blessings in the past but I couldn't receive them because of the negative person I had become, but now I can see every single gift, each time that I opened my eyes and breath, the opportunity to live one more day and make a difference in someone's life. I'm obligated to encourage, inspire and love, this is my mission, and I am bound to help others towards understanding the meaning of a purposeful life. At some point we all come to a place and space that we begin to seek a higher understanding. We live out our lives as being an example of the betterment of what we took for granted. My past would not allow me to unwrap every day and appreciate how precious every moment was meant to be until I understood my purpose. This journey I began in the womb my life didn't become transparent until the day I lost my father, the day I finally understood that each day that I was blessed to wake up and open my eyes and see the beauty in everything. Once I understood this each day I embraced would be like Christmas morning excited, happy and full of joy. Each day that I'm given I would wake up not knowing what good things would be given to me without asking, but these things are called blessings, receiving God's favor. You don't know what to expect but you would pray that each new day would be the best day ever. It's such a good feeling that it felt like butterflies in your stomach, eagerly awaiting for the unknown to bring forth a surprise, the anticipation of receiving something but not sure what is the most beautiful feeling you will ever experience. Once you receive it, it's like opening a birthday present or something you've wished for, it's the inside of the box that keeps you in a happy frame of mind, you smile until you open it, sometimes it would be what you hoped for and sometimes it would have something inside you weren't expecting but either way I would make the choice for happiness.

Now at times you can receive something you didn't want but you had to make it work, and sometimes God will tell us no, but that no only means not right now! This is how God works. I came to understand how and what faith is supposed to be, it's like magic if you believed and applied what happens next would be magical. My darkest hours would always bring about the greatest messages and lessons. I began to see all the wrong choices and decision I had made in my life beginning to haunt me, the consequences of my past delivered my greatest pain but yet it created my most beautiful moments. This pain would never be re-visited again it would merely be housed deep within my spirit to fuel my quest of living out my dreams in order to live my best life boldly, to stand in my truth and believe in my faith no matter what. I had to stop driving myself crazy trying to understand why something happened and understand it was what my soul needed to grow. I came to understand that every event that happened in my life was preparing me for exactly what I ask. The very thing that I feared was the very thing that set me free. Every closed door brought forth a bigger blessing, every bad event fueled my determination, every lie that was told raised me higher, every enemy became the reason why I smile. Every storm that came taught me patience until the path was cleared, my next chapter has been written I waiting to step in.

Absolutely nothing goes wrong in the journey of life, there's a reason for all things and circumstances. I now understand that the results behind mistakes that are made will be the lessons or the message that I need to pay attention to. Trust the process always, everyday of our lives there will be tests presented to determine the integrity of the human spirit, our choices determine the karma. In order to get what you've never had you must become what you've never been and in order to gain understanding you must be willing to go where you've never gone.

I began to learn how to stay in the moment and not be moved by troubles. I began to learn how to have inner peace with the assurance that all things work together for the good. I've learned that everything that was against me was for me, I had to learn how to stand on every promise of God. He has delivered me out of every wrong situation and He gave me unspeakable joy, He taught me how not to be anxious for nothing, I learned how to assign a scripture to every situation and to lean not on my own understanding but rather trust in the Lord with all things. I've learned how not to allow fear, negativity, and hurtful things to control me but rather focus on the opportunities to further strengthen my faith and to seek God's strength and will for my life.

The beauty of a butterfly is never replicated, you will never see the same butterfly or it's beauty ever again once its purpose has been fulfilled and this would be the same for human life. What most do not understand about the caterpillar is that once they enter into their cocoon and begin the process of metamorphosis nothing will stop the creation of the butterfly and the same applies to us. What's for you will get, nothing will stop the process of you obtaining it. If anything henders the process of the caterpillar it will cease to exist and die. The same would apply for us.

Change is a magnificent process of life creating life and each time this process is completed the Universe nevers replicates the same pattern of beauty. It's and the same process happens with human life. Life will always make a way to evolve, recreate, and come back more vibrant and beautiful than before.

One must understand that life will bring together what's meant to happen for you but you must trust every aspect of the process. Everything that I experienced in my life, everything that I went through was necessary and it has brought forward a woman that's ready to live out all of her dreams and live life unapologetically. My father's transition brought about the absolute best of my life I thought that losing my father would cause me to drift throughout life upset, mad, angry at the world for something that was already written in my father's script that has now been transformed and infused into my lifescript. You either decided to wander and be lost or you decide to begin living. Unbeknownst to me, my father's death brought forward the most beautiful gift a daughter could possibly receive and that gift would be my life as I've come to understand it and I'll never allow anyone or anything to rob me of the love that was promised to me long ago. Standing in my truth and acknowledging my endless possibilities every single day while the necessity of everything in my life continues to amaze me!

CHAPTER SEVEN

7 Purposeful Gifts

"If any of you lacks wisdom, he should ask God,
who gives generously to all without finding fault
and it will be given to him" —James 1:5

1 Corinthians 12 (NIV, 2017), speaks of the seven (7) spiritual gifts of the Holy Spirit; wisdom, intellect, counsel, fortitude, knowledge, piety and fear of the Lord.

1. **Wisdom** is considered the first and the greatest of these gifts.
2. **Intellect** (aka understanding) is a perceptive intuition which magnifies the mind to grasp the truths of faith
3. **Counsel** is the perception of supernatural intuition, it enables a person to judge promptly and rightly, especially in difficult situations.
4. **Fortitude** is often identified with courage, it's described as a willingness to stand up for what is right in the sight of God, even if it means accepting rejection, verbal abuse, or physical harm. The gift of fortitude allows individuals the firmness of the mind that is required in doing both good and in enduring evil.
5. **Knowledge** the gift of knowledge allows one, as far as is humanly possible to see things from God's perspective. It allows us to perceive the greatness of God and his love for his creatures through creation.
6. **Piety** accords with reverence. A person with reverence recognizes his total reliance on God and comes before God with humility, trust, and love.
7. **Fear of the Lord**

I've come to the realization that everything in life has rules there isn't one thing that we make a decision and or choice to do that does not come with rules or laws that we must abide by,

65

however, what's interesting is that people are more concerned with man's rules and laws than God's. These gifts are all given to believers of the same spirit, and God decides which gift that will manifest through your spirit.

Throughout the Bible, God incorporates the number seven (7). At the beginning of the Bible the number 7 is identified with things being completed or finished. In the book of Revelation, the number 7 is used more than fifty times in a variety of contexts. The number 7 is used in the Bible more than seven hundred times and in order to understand the intended purpose for your life, one must possess one of the seven spiritual gifts of the spirit and live in truth & faith. Then and only then will your script become revealed to you for your intended purpose. The seven (7) spiritual gifts of the Holy Spirit are available to all who believe and follow God's instructions. These seven (7) essential rules, you should live in accordance to their instructions in order for God to reveal your purpose.

When you are able to stand fervently in truth and believe in your faith the impossible will become possible, locked doors will be opened, and your desires will fall into fruition.

When you can love and forgive your enemies in spite of what they've done, only then will you be truly prepared to be elevated into your next season. You have to put a down payment on what's to come next in your life, meaning you should commit yourself to knowing and understanding your purpose, following the instructions of God and live as honestly as possible. We all must pay our dues before the cow can be taken home. What most don't understand is failure can become one of your greatest teachers only if you know how to unlearn from previous behaviors and experiences. You must learn how to lose well in order to truly appreciate winning, you don't become a winner unless you have had some losses. Once you understand these basic principles no one will be able to defeat you they may beat you, but never defeat you, only you can allow yourself to be defeated mentally, spiritually or emotionally.

Matthew 5:4 instructs us to love our enemies and those who opposed or cause harm. One of the greatest feelings in the world is knowing that you have grown spiritually when words from the enemy are said to harm you but they do not move you this is the moment you realize that you have matured and grown into your spiritual truth. Wisdom speaks truth, evil speaks harm.

The storms of life are inevitable, these are required to define and determine your character, that will build strength but in order to survive and obtain the meaning to the trails (aka tests), you must demonstrate your will before God, He wants to see what your endurance is made of, He wants to determine your strength, He wants to see what your faith is is made of, therefore, if you place your confidence and trust in God and lean on Him for absolutely everything and trust the process always the trails of life will not harm you. The bible has provided numerous examples of how to endure lost, how to survive pain, how to gain knowledge and learn from mistakes, it instructs us to trust and believe, how to love, how to be the example, however, we are the ones that decides our plan is a better plan, we are the ones who decides to fix the problem only to make matters worse.

If we truly lived as Job, if we truly trust God as Daniel these tests will not cause you to be disrupted they will build your aptness that will show Him your faithfulness. To do this you must create a direct connection with God you must incorporate a strong prayer life and understand that prayer is one of the most essential keys towards having a direct dialogue with God.

The Universe protects those who are faithful and loyal in spirit, God will truly make your enemies your footstool, He will change and turn a situation meant to harm you into a bigger blessing. But in order to possess this type of power you must be resilient towards sin you must rebuke wrong doings. The battle between good and evil exists is real and this fight will be among us until the end of time, and if we do as instructed you can live amongst the shadows and have a beautiful life and be blessed with all the desires of your heart. What makes living complicated is our own selfishness that turns into dark and demonic needs with an agenda to hurt or harm others, but if you are in the will of the Universe, you will be protected from harm. He has given us all free will to make the right choices and choose to follow the instructions freely, He has stated that His word be practiced and followed on a daily basis this allows us to remain connected to God's instructions for our lives, it's impossible to follow Him without having unshakable faith.

So often we complain that God doesn't hear us or He doesn't answer our prayers, and when our minds have become polluted with the toxic voices of the wrong people our vision becomes distorted and our reality will quickly turn into the reality of what others create for us and we begin to live in their world versus our own. The lack of money, happiness, love, self-respect, will expose you to dangerous waters, and you will lose sight of the script that God has written for your life. In order for a television to work it must be plugged in to receive electricity, in order for cars to run it must be filled with gas, in order to understand you must seek the knowledge, in order to receive you must watch and wait for God's timing. God only reveals Himself to us when we are connected into His word and we follow His instructions. As we wait patiently and listen for the instructions keep in mind that the tests and storms will come but the question to you is how will you wait?

The woman that I'm becoming continues to amaze me, therefore, I'm obligated to move according to the script intended for my life. When you make a mistake or make a bad choice you can't go back and correct or erase it, life isn't a time capsule, but what we can do is forgive ourselves and learn from it. Once you know better and the lesson has been learned now you must apply wisdom to the events that present in your life. The seasons and weather should be our teachers as to how change is inevitable and even though the storms may bring devastation we must trust the process, we must learn how to rebuild or reinvent ourselves and believe the outcomes will be greater than we could possibly imagine. It's said that if you want to make God laugh, tell Him your plans!

We will never be able to change the mistakes or the insecure admiration of others it's been said that life is extremely short so don't allow the misrepresentation of yourself to defeat or prevent you for living the happiest life possible. The power of forgiveness will free you, it will remove the strongholds, and you will begin to embrace your purpose, the power forgiving yourself and others will open your eyes to the beauty of all things. Forgiveness is a gift that most don't have nor do they give it but once you understand the power in this word you'll begin to see life so much more clearer and the things and people who once were ugly will become beautiful. Give someone the gift of forgiveness but most importantly be a gift to yourself. Always trust the process, don't question it, don't turn away, just trust and believe. All things are possible if you only believe! Know when it's time to turn the page, sometimes we skip pages or chapters and we close the book without understanding the narrative. Watch for the signs and ask for understanding, embrace the lessons, gain the knowledge of your life. What you fear the most will be the very thing that will set you free! Come to understand **The Necessity of All Things!**

Where to contact the author...

If you would like to contact Allenda for media interviews or speaking engagements you may contact her at the following addresses:

Email: letsconnect@gmail.com

Facebook: Everything is Necessary or @towardsconnectingtoone

Twitter: letsconnect

Instragram:@thenecessityofallthings

YouTube: Lets Connect One to One

If you would like to share your story of how you discovered your purpose please send your information to one of the above addresses.

www.ingramcontent.com/pod-product-compliance
Lightning Source LLC
Chambersburg PA
CBHW031218120626
46545CB00003B/896